All of life is sermon prep. But it's hard for preachers to know how to let God use our lives without making our sermons about us. With pastoral wisdom, Steve Norman describes ten different roles that the preacher plays, inviting the kind of spiritual development and self-awareness that will allow readers to discern how to let sermons grow from their own discipleship.

MANDY SMITH, Pastor at University Christian Church in Cincinnati, OH and author of *Unfettered: Imagining a Childlike Faith Beyond the Baggage of Western Culture* & *The Vulnerable Pastor*

Steve Norman beautifully reminds us that life change must first happen in the communicator before it can happen in the congregation. Norman offers us a manual for all who teach or preach, showing us how the messenger is the message and what we say must transform our hearts and minds before it can transform others. The Preacher as Sermon *is a must-read book for preachers that preaches to the preacher!*

DAVE FERGUSON, Lead Pastor, Community Christian Church (Naperville, IL) and author of *B.L.E.S.S. 5 Everyday Ways to Love Your Neighbor* and *Change the World*

Steve Norman is one of those rare artists who not only masters his craft but thinks deeply about mastery itself. There are master carpenters who know their trade intuitively, but oddly they can't explain how to cut a mortise joint with a good router. They just do it. There are other carpenters who do this as well but know how to bring others along. They know what we do not know and what we need to know.

Steve's The Preacher As Sermon *is one of those books that gives us some of the secrets to gaining that elusive mastery of the pulpit. He doesn't presume perfection but shows what he's learned in his own journey. In ten chapters Steve develops the truth of one controlling idea: "There's a direct line between the state of our soul and the tenor of truth proclaimed." That is, how we are formed on the inside will indicate how we speak on the outside.*

This will determine if we speak from a metaphorical "tall pulpit" or from "among" our audiences. Whether we see ourselves as "co-travelers" with our audiences or priests who make few personal discoveries. These attitudes happen subconsciously but here Steve helps us bring them out into the open, reimagine them, and reform them so that we will preach differently. This book is a gift to all of us and will richly reward careful reading.

GARY M. BURGE, Professor of New Testament and Dean of the Faculty at Calvin Theological Seminary (Grand Rapids, MI)

This book stands on its own among those found in the preaching genre of your favorite online bookseller. Dialogue about the nuanced techniques for proclaiming the Word of God has its place, of course, but Steve maintains that a preacher's most consistent and ongoing private formation—separate from any ministerial witness to others—fundamentally influences long-term sustainability and gospel effectiveness. In short, those who don't seek God's help to address their personality hiccups, maladaptive tendencies, family traumas, and fears will inevitably renounce core aspects of the faithful, fruitful freedom in Christ that God intends, including but not limited to their preaching.

For preachers, it is easy for us to hide behind the pulpit as "a resounding gong or a clanging cymbal" (1 Cor. 13:1). Too many pastoral leaders are inauthentic and anemic regarding their own spiritual formation—the various disciplines and graces needed to be, first, in meaningful communion with God—which is a crisis Steve rightly addresses as only a preacher can, one to another. To preach is a high calling, yes, but none who do it are higher than the One who placed the divine phone call to begin with.

For those with ears to hear and eyes to see anew, Steve reminds us of this and much more. If you are a preacher, aspire to be one, or are a layperson interested in the inner workings of the preachers in your life, grab a copy.

JAMES ELLIS III, author of *Tell the Truth, Shame the Devil: Stories about the Challenges of Young Pastors* (www.JamesEllis3.com) (Langley, British Columbia)

Preachers, preaching students, and those who listen to preachers will benefit from Steve Norman's exploration of the multi-faceted role of the preacher as an artist, joy-generator, fellow-sufferer, fellow-traveler, and more. You can trust Steve to remind you what preaching is and who it's ultimately about.

Of the many roles Steve explores, he returns again and again to the preacher's identity as God's beloved child, where we receive freedom and peace. If you want to explore how a preacher is spiritually formed to preach without shame, self-promotion, or self-protection, this is the book for you. It's one of those books a preacher needs to read regularly.

SARA BARTON, Pepperdine University Chaplain (Malibu, CA)

I like this book. It has something for new preachers and old. Without rejecting homiletical technique, it starts with something prior. It starts at the very beginning—a very good place to start—with the preacher's calling, role(s), and soul. We are sons/daughters, listeners, travelers, intercessors, artists, coaches, and so forth. I was challenged by the reminder that we are joy-generators.

JEFFREY ARTHURS, Professor of Preaching and Communication & Chair, Division of Practical Theology at Gordon-Conwell Theological Seminary (Hamilton, MA).

This book addresses a critical need. The unintended consequence of the proliferation of "ready-to-preach" materials are passable sermons, while the soul of the preacher withers and evaporates. Is this an underlying cause of the pastoral burnout increasingly common today?

It is written not with condemnation, but life-giving direction—a source of vitality in the pastor and in the pulpit. Norman is right, "we are called to be wordsmiths and theologians. And we are called to be stewards and gardeners." In his book he walks alongside us in that garden path. And the overflow is transformative for the spiritually lost and the seasoned saints.

WAYNE SCHMIDT, General Superintendent, The Wesleyan Church (Fishers, IN)

To the making of preaching books, there is no end. Yet I'm thrilled that Steve Norman has contributed a homiletical gem with this important resource for preachers and teachers of God's Word. The Pastor as Sermon *is infused with wisdom garnered from decades of pastoral experience. Norman understands that the act of preaching cannot be separated from the person of the preacher. Presenting ten carefully selected characteristics, he presents a balanced perspective on what it means for preachers to embody their sermons for their congregations. And reminding us that preaching is a delight, Norman showcases the beauty of preaching and the beauty of persons who faithfully proclaim the Word.*

> **MATTHEW D. KIM,** George F. Bennett Chair of Practical Theology, Director of the Haddon W. Robinson Center for Preaching, Gordon-Conwell Theological Seminary (Hamilton, MA); author of *Preaching with Cultural Intelligence* and *Preaching to People in Pain*

With the care and precision of a surgeon Steve Norman examines both the craft and art of preaching. A student of homiletics, Norman takes us on a journey, looking at what we preachers do, through ten lenses. Quoting a wide variety of thinkers from C. S. Lewis to Betty Edwards to Pete Scazzero to Dr. Seuss, Steve dares us to improve our preaching, to become less mechanical and more artistic, and to think about what we are doing. Giving us free sermon outlines along the way, Norman teases us as he hints at how we could approach a text, all the while daring us to be better next Sunday than we were last. If you're a "three alliterative points and a poem" preacher, this book is not for you. If you're a hungry, holy homiletician, this well-thought out, practical volume is a delight.

> **RICHARD ALLAN FARMER,** Pastor at Crossroads Presbyterian Church (Stone Mountain, GA)

THE Preacher AS Sermon

How Who You Are Shapes What They Hear

STEVE NORMAN

The Preacher as Sermon: How Who You Are Shapes What They Hear

Published by Christianity Today
465 Gundersen Drive, Carol Stream, IL 60188

Printed in the U.S.A.

PreachingToday.com

Publisher: Rob Toal
Editorial: Andrew Finch, Jim Bolton, Alex Mellen
Marketing: Todd Watermann, Kelsey Bowse
Design: Jillian Hathaway
Author Photo: DJ Hurula

Cover Image: Lampost Collective / Lightstock

To my Dad and Mom, Renny and Catherine Norman,
for your unflinching prayers and constant encouragement,
for modeling a journey of faithfulness, and for giving me tools to
believe boldly, think critically, and speak clearly.

Foreword

Preaching is about who before it is ever about what or how.

The Who of preaching is first and foremost God, the one Who in the perfect communion of the Father, Son, and Spirit communicates the world into existence; Who speaks the word to Adam and Eve, Abraham, Moses, and Israel; Who as the Living Word, Jesus Christ, communes and communicates God's redeeming love and justice; and Who through the presence and power of the Holy Spirit addresses and fills God's people, Who are then to be ambassadors of the Evangel for the sake of the world.

The biblical narrative is focused on Who from beginning to culmination. Who is the most important revelation in the Bible, and Who is therefore the most important question about those who live and speak about Who. Throughout the Old and New Testament, call is centered in Who calls, and only then about who is called. The meaning of human life flows directly from the breath of the one Who marks us with the divine image. The hope that Abram holds onto is about Who calls him to go to a far place. Likewise, Moses speaks and acts with power entirely because God has called and anointed him to be Yahweh's divine embodiment to lead God's people. This continues through various men and women, through the kings and the prophets, the rich and the poor, those with power and without.

The greatest underscoring of Who is the one Who comes in human flesh to incarnate the Word of God, Jesus Christ. He is not comely, or powerful, or obvious. This Who is to be seen and heard, even if the real, embodied presence of God does not come with trumpets and spectacle but with an unexpected, understated presence: "Who, being in very nature God, did not consider equality with God something to be used to his own advantage; rather, he made himself nothing by taking the very nature of a servant, being made in human likeness. And being found in appearance as a man, he humbled himself by becoming obedient to death—even death on a cross!" (Phil. 2:6–8). This is our clearest picture of God. "Therefore God exalted him to the highest place and gave him the name that is above every name, that at the name of Jesus every knee should bow, in heaven and on earth and under the earth, and every tongue acknowledge that Jesus Christ is Lord, to the glory of God the Father" (vv. 9–11).

The Who of God is not yet finished being made known and experienced until in wind, fire, and tongues, the Holy Spirit comes to be our Inner Teacher, Comforter, Fire, and Guide. We are to show Who we serve and worship by lives expressing, enacting, and exuding the presence of God's love, grace, truth, and justice. The Who of God—Father, Son, and Spirit—provides gifts so that the who of the body of Christ looks, and smells, and sounds, and acts like the Who that calls them into one humanity.

The church is meant to be the new who in the world, a communion of unlike people who find themselves and each other by being found by the Who that draws us to God's self, and therefore to share a new life in union with God in Christ by the Spirit for the sake of the world. The Who that is God creates a new who that is the church, the unlikeliest of whos.

For this body to grow and mature, to gather in God's living presence and to experience together God's life making us new, we need more than anything else to hear God's ongoing speech to us by the living Word, through the written Word, delivered by the preached Word. And again, the central issue is who: Who is the preacher to God? Who is God to the preacher? Who is the preacher living for? Who is shaping the heart, mind, and will of the preacher? Whose voice is the preacher seeking to hear most? Who are the voices that are the loudest in the preacher's ears? Who are the people the preacher seeks to serve? Who does the preacher aim to serve?

Who are those people in their world? Who are they seeking to be and whose affirmation means the most to them?

These questions literally go on endlessly through the narrative of the Bible and the life of the people of God. Who the people of God become is often a reflection of the preachers in their lives. Thus, the who of the preacher will be one of the most influential voices.

In an era of technique and technology, preaching can be stripped or masked of its God-intended, visceral reality. When hearing a preacher for the first time, our best instincts lead us to ask: Who is this talking? What can I discern from what and how they are communicating that conveys to me who they really are and in who or what is their life truly grounded? From whom or what does this preacher draw life, or truth, or wisdom? Which who most defines and directs this preacher's life? Who we are is manifest in our being and our doing. So when the preacher speaks, we are exposed to both. This is not about any requirement or anticipation of appearance, but about reality. Of course, we can be easily distracted by the former, but it will be the latter that we need.

The gift of this book by Steve Norman is that it explores all of these dimensions involved in the who of preaching. His work here shows experience, humility, assurance, openness, growth, and more. The who that is Steve Norman is here, and that is a very good thing for all of this book's readers. From the time we first met, I had the sense that Steve hungered for the reality of God in his own life, in his preaching, in his church leadership, and in his life in the world. We have walked together for a number of years now, and my initial instinct has only been confirmed. I read this book with gratitude and with pleasure, with conviction and with hunger, in the hope that who he is and what he is saying is what I, and every preacher I know, needs in varying ways.

Preaching is about Who and who from start to finish. That is its wonder and mystery.

MARK LABBERTON | President, Fuller Seminary

Contents

Acknowledgements 15

Introduction: On Flower Beds 17

Chapter 1: The Preacher As Defined by Scripture 21

Chapter 2: The Preacher As Son/Daughter 35

Chapter 3: The Preacher As Listener 47

Chapter 4: The Preacher As Fellow Traveler 57

Chapter 5: The Preacher As Intercessor 71

Chapter 6: The Preacher As Artist 83

Chapter 7: The Preacher As Coach 97

Chapter 8: The Preacher As Joy-Generator 109

Chapter 9: The Preacher As Pipeline 119

Chapter 10: The Preacher As Fellow Sufferer 127

Conclusion: A Box of Hats 137

Acknowledgments

To Christ, the Author and Perfector of our faith. I can only love because you first loved me, and I can only speak because you called my name.

To my parents and siblings. Thanks for shaping me into who I am.

Cathy Norman-Petersen, you have been helping me edit my thoughts since I was in middle school. Thanks for pushing me to write and publishing my first pieces.

Andrew Finch: Your encouragement and patience helped me to establish my feet as a writer to pastors and leaders. This project wouldn't be complete without your mastery, tenacity, and wisdom.

Jim Bolton, Jillian Hathaway, Alex Mellen, Todd Watermann, Rob Toal, and Kelsey Bowse: Thank you to the Preaching Today team for believing in this project and thank you for all of your help editing, designing, and marketing the book.

Kyle Rohane, Ryan Pazdur, Londa Alderink, Mike Salisbury: Thanks for the books, the kind words, the lunches, and coffees, and your commitment to the craft of writing.

Mark Labberton: Thanks for your unwavering commitment to preachers and preaching. I am who am I because of your example and your work.

To preachers who shaped me, both directly and indirectly: Erwin McManus, Jay Kesler, Bob Schmidgall, Richard Allen Farmer, Jack Sara, Baruch Maoz, Akiva Cohen, Ramesh Sapkota, Harvey Carey, Gary Burge, Jennifer Ackerman, Sara Barton, Michelle Erickson, Salim Munayer, Billy Graham, Phil Collins, and Ken Davis.

To the Micah Groups in Detroit, thanks for helping me see how much I have yet to learn.

To the preachers who are early on their journeys: Caleb Maxon,

Mason Rosado, Xiamary Moreno, McCaila Andrews, Bre Harris. Your voices are gifts to the church and to me. Keep lifting them up.

To my amazing church families in Royal Oak, Troy, and Holland, Michigan. Thank for trusting me with your time and your hearts.

To Kelly, for walking this wild road with me. I can only do what I do because I get to do it with you. Your courage and wisdom, your heart for God and the church, your love for me and our family is the greatest gift I could ask for.

Grace, Naomi, Josiah, Mariam—All of my best stories come from you, your faith, and your love for life. In the end, the only sermon I care about is the one you watch me live.

Introduction

On Flower Beds

On my desk, there's a Bible, a spiral notebook, a ball-point pen, and a copy of *Illustrations for Preaching and Teaching*. In my soul, a passion to preach. In my mind, the memories of sermons I have heard that have shaped me. I'm in college, and these are the only tools I know to use for preaching. Over the next decade, my toolbox grows to include formal education, public speaking workshops, ministry conferences, and more books. Many, many books.

The quantum leaps in technology increase access to the number of preaching tools we have and the speed at which we can reach them. There was an era when you could gauge a preacher's experience by looking at the shelves in his or her study. That era is gone. The toolbox can't fit on our shelves anymore; it's boundless.

And yet, this vast toolbox is limited; preaching is more than the capability to internalize and repeat information. It transcends the ability to synthesize constructs and contextualize concepts. Preaching eclipses our cognitive capacity. Compelling preaching is visceral. It sweats and bleeds with the hearer and weeps and rejoices with the text. It requires the preacher to embody and express a spiritual pulse, a holy heartbeat.

Preachers don't need more tricks and tips; we need help cultivating a life that generates great sermons. We have seen, and been, people who have studied, even mastered, the finer points of homiletics, timing, diction, and delivery, and still had sermons fall flat. And we've seen messengers who lacked training and technique preach words that bring us to our very knees.

Why? Because there's something that doesn't happen in the study that informs our preaching. There's a direct line between the state of our soul and the tenor of truth proclaimed. Yes, the Word stands beyond and above us, but it's being spoken through us.

The preacher's formation shapes the preacher's preaching. How I live influences how I preach and how I don't. Who I am shapes what I will say and what I won't. Jesus says, "Each tree is recognized by its own fruit. People do not pick figs from thornbushes, or grapes from briers. A good man brings good things out of the good stored up in his heart, and an evil man brings evil things out of the evil stored up in his heart. For the mouth speaks what the heart is full of." (Luke 6:44–45).

It's easier for me to spend time toying with the preaching toolbox than it is to tend my heart and prune my soul. But as preachers, we neglect our interior world at our peril. Yes, we are wordsmiths and theologians. And we are called to be stewards and gardeners.

I like to think of preaching like a garden. Beautiful gardens have perennials and annuals. Perennials are the preaching themes that are core to me. They're ingrained in my psyche; they are truths and texts I always come back to. Annuals are seasonal. They are thoughts, struggles, and questions that are fresh to me in the unique moment I'm preparing to preach. Annuals are shaped by my life-stage, my current spiritual journey, and the trials and triumphs of the people I'm speaking to. So, when you're going to preach, go to your garden and pick a fresh bouquet, a mix of where you've been and where you are, to give to people when you preach. This bouquet-based perspective on preaching is dynamic. It views the preacher and the preaching as an integrated ecosystem: a living, breathing, generative whole.

In their work *Art and Fear,* David Bayles and Ted Orland write, "There's a difference between meaning that is embodied and meaning that is referenced."[1] At various points in our walk as preachers, we reference the meaning we've studied, received, and observed. But on our best days, we embody that meaning and it's the extension of our identity and the overflow of our spiritual life. The authors continue, "The hardest part of artmaking is living your life in such a way that your work gets done, over and over—and that means, among other things, finding a host of practices that are just plain useful."[2]

For me, the hardest part of preaching isn't the preparation, serving as a local church pastor, or the relentless weekly grind. It's living my life in such a way that gives birth to good preaching. Of course, the scriptures have much to say about the aim and the art of preaching, so our journey will start there. But once we've established how the Bible defines "preacher," I want to explore the varying roles we preachers play.

There has been more than one season when I've been stuck in my preaching. And in those moments, when I've wrestled with my call, my doubts, my fatigue, or even my church, it's been helpful for me to reframe how I view myself. I need to remember that:

- Before I'm a preacher, I'm child of God.
- Before I'm a speaker, I must be a listener.

---

[1] Dave Bayles and Ted Orland, *Art and Fear: Observations on the Perils (and Rewards) of Artmaking* (Santa Cruz, CA: The Image Continuum, 1993), 55.
[2] Ibid, 61.

- Before I'm a guide, I must be a fellow traveler.
- As I'm an interlocutor, I'm an intercessor.
- As I'm a theologian, I'm an artist.
- As I lift my voice, I'm a coach and mentor to current and future voices.
- As I experience joy, I'm a joy-generator to others.
- As I receive truth, I'm a pipeline through which it flows.
- As I witness the suffering of others, I'm a fellow sufferer asking God to redeem our hurts.

We are all of these and more. We're not sermon-writing machines and human megaphones; we are wells out of which the Spirit draws water to quench thirsty people. Join me on a journey as we explore what kind of life generates life-giving preaching.

1

The Preacher As Defined by Scripture

I live in Holland, Michigan, a town with a deep appreciation for its Dutch immigrant roots. Holland loves its parades; there are three days of spectacle at their annual Tulip Time every May. The one constant? Every parade begins with the town crier, John Karsten, at the front. He leads the crowd in full historic regalia, complete with a big tricorn hat and white gloves. John rings his hand bell with a flourish as he walks down Eighth Street declaring, "Hear ye, hear ye . . ." followed by the specific declaration of the day.

John's been doing this for 40 years. He owns his role as town herald. Locals and tourists can tell he loves it. He's got something to say and he's going to say it. When a local news anchor asked, "Did you have to get special training to be the town crier?" he replied with a wink and smile, "You just have to have a big mouth."

John doesn't crash these parades. He's formally deputized by the city to lead them. If you're a preacher, in any capacity, you're a town crier too. You've been equipped, empowered, released, and charged to call people to a clear understanding of Christ.

In Colossians 1:28–29, Paul notes, "He is the one we proclaim, admonishing and teaching everyone with all wisdom, so that we may present everyone fully mature in Christ. To this end I strenuously contend with all the energy Christ so powerfully works in me." Paul comes to the preaching moment with confidence (he's playing the herald), intelligence (he's teaching with all wisdom), focus (he wants it to result in maturity), sweat (he contends strenuously), and passion (fueled by energy sparked by Christ himself).

Preaching, as described in Scripture, is far more dynamic than merely "giving a talk" or "delivering a presentation." A long list of prepositions and nouns follow the word *preach* in the Bible. The Scriptures don't just nod in the direction of the call to preach; they give us the what, the why, the where, and the how of preaching.

The following speaks to the tone of preaching in contexts of *against* and *repentance*. We will also look at the content of our preaching, as we explore words like *him, Christ crucified,* and *peace*. We will address the audience in unique places with words like *to* and *among*. And we will touch on the motive of preaching with a simple adverb: *voluntarily*. A brief overview of the scriptural phrases that include "preaching ______" gives a compelling, multidimensional picture of how preaching works.

Tone of Our Preaching

'Against'

Preaching happens in specific places to unique people practicing observable actions. The preacher is called to preach against places that exhibit rebellion against God's character and purposes. The admonition to preach against a place is frequent for the prophets. It occurs twice in Ezekiel:

> "Son of man, set your face toward the south; preach against the south and prophesy against the forest of the southland." (Ezek. 20:46)

Ezekiel goes on to describe the imminent destruction by fire of the forest and the region:

> "The word of the Lord came to me: 'Son of man, set your face against Jerusalem and preach against the sanctuary. Prophesy against the land of Israel.' " (Ezek. 21:1-2)

Then he explains that the king of Babylon will lay siege to the city and defeat it, resulting in a Jewish exile.

A lazy reading of Ezekiel portrays a vindictive God drunk on destruction. The thread that runs through Ezekiel, however, is restoration. Yes, God's judgment is the "what" of Ezekiel, but the "why" of said judgment is to ultimately reconcile a rebellious people back to God. It's to unite the runaway bride to the faithful groom. There's a phrase that appears over 60 times in Ezekiel—"they will know that I am the Lord." The motive behind the judgment is revelation. Once the people see that God is in fact Jehovah, they will be prompted to turn to him.

To preach "against" isn't vindictive scolding. It's not a self-righteous reprimand, but a clear and firm invitation for the prodigal to return home.

Just as God calls Ezekiel to preach against Israel, he calls Jonah to preach against Assyria:

> "Go to the great city of Nineveh and preach against it, because its wickedness has come up before me." (Jonah 1:2)

Jonah understands that underlying the "preach against" motif is a bedrock of mercy. This is precisely why his first instinct is to resist the mission. When he finally does go, and Nineveh responds with repentance, Jonah sulks because God never unleashed the fury the Assyrians deserved. It's easy to look back and call Jonah a temperamental brat.

However, Jonah's hostility toward the Assyrians is personal. When Assyria attacked Samaria, they came from the north, through Galilee, where Jonah is reportedly from. It's possible Jonah had friends, relatives, or neighbors who were, at best, taken in captivity to Nineveh or, at worst, slain in the invasion. Jonah doesn't despise the Assyrians in the abstract; he hates them in practice.

Preaching against your enemies, those individuals or groups who have done you wrong, is easy when you despise them. But that's never the tone in which it's supposed to occur. Preaching against must be rooted in compassion, a deep love for an often-hostile audience, and consistency, a life without hypocrisy.

This is why Paul asks the following in his letter to the Romans: "You, then, who teach others, do you not teach yourself? You who preach against stealing, do you steal?" (Rom. 2:21). Paul affirms preaching against stealing (a behavior), but such preaching lacks credibility if the preacher is a thief. God's call to the prophets is to preach against with compassion, and Paul's demand for the preacher is to preach against with integrity.

'Repentance'

There was a season in my life when I only associated preaching repentance with wild-eyed sidewalk prophets wearing sandwich board signs with fear-based evangelistic slogans on them like "Turn or Burn."

Yet when I look at the Gospels, the admonition to repent isn't accompanied by high-volume threats. Rather, the invitation to repent is usually accompanied by a declaration of the kingdom's goodness. The message, then, isn't "Repent: Hell is hot." It's "Repent: The kingdom is close. And it's amazing."

Matthew indicates Jesus begins to preach repentance immediately following his wilderness experience: "From that time on Jesus began to preach, 'Repent, for the kingdom of heaven has come near' " (Matt. 4:17). Later he explains that Jesus' proclamation of the good news of the kingdom is accompanied by signs of healing and deliverance.

To preach repentance must include a compelling "why," and it's that life in the light and wonder of the kingdom that eclipses life in the dark on our own.

Jesus' disciples follow this model as well. Mark 6:12–13 says, "They went out and preached that people should repent. They drove out many demons and anointed many sick people with oil and healed them." The call to repent can come with a smile, not a scowl, because the invitation is couched in concrete examples of God's grace, kindness, and power.

We repent to follow a good God, who makes people whole and sets people free. The aim of repentance is proximity to God, not avoiding judgment. Paul says as much in Romans 2:4: "Or do you show contempt for the riches of his kindness, forbearance and patience, not realizing that God's kindness is intended to lead you to repentance?" and John confirms this in 1 John 4:18, "There is no fear in love. But perfect love drives out fear, because fear has to do with punishment."

Content of Our Preaching

'The Word/Gospel'

Evangelistic preaching begins with an invitation to repent and believe. In Jesus' ministry this is then followed by a more thorough explanation of the nature of God and the kingdom. When Jesus returns to Capernaum after traveling to the surrounding villages, crowds flock to see him.

> "They gathered in such large numbers that there was no room left, not even outside the door, and he preached the word to them." (Mark 2:2)

When Paul encourages Timothy to preach, he's clear about the content. He says, with typically Pauline directness, "Preach the word" (2 Tim. 4:2).

In a church in which I served, one of the preachers told the story of a friend who was an itinerant speaker at churches, camps, and conferences. The speaker once told the pastor, "I've got a great message. I just need some verses to go with it." There's nothing wrong with speaking that encourages and inspires people, but it's not in the same category as preaching the Word. Both Jesus and Paul start with the Word and move to their audience.

If *Word* is one common noun that follows *preach* in Scripture, *gospel* is the other.

In Acts 16, Paul and his friends are eagerly trying to determine where they should proclaim the message of Jesus next. They try to "preach the word" in Asia but are unable to do so (v. 6). They attempt in Bithynia, but the path is blocked (v. 7). In this season, Paul receives a vision from a Macedonian man begging for help. Acts 16:10 says, "After Paul had seen the vision, we got ready at once to leave for Macedonia, concluding that God had called us to preach the gospel to them." For Paul, everywhere he went, the bedrock of preaching was the same: the Word, the gospel.

I used to think that preaching the gospel was primarily for those who are new to, or young in, the faith. The more I lean into my own faith journey, however, the more I appreciate the breadth, width, and depth of the gospel. The gospel isn't the threshold message that gets us into advanced spiritual truths; it is the capstone that holds all the other threads and themes of Scripture together.

'Him'

Colossians 1:17 says, "[Christ] is before all things, and in him all things hold together." When we preach, we always preach Christ. We don't have to wedge the person of Christ into every passage. Every time we preach, though, is an opportunity to remind our hearers that Christ is present in every moment and intervening in every circumstance.

Paul tells the Galatians his primary message is a person, Christ revealed to him, not a precept or principle. "But when God, who set me apart from my mother's womb and called me by his grace, was pleased to reveal his Son in me so that I might preach him among the Gentiles, my immediate response was not to consult any human being" (Gal. 1:15–16).

Writer David Brooks contends John Stott captured the essence of what it means to simply "preach him":

> [John] Stott's mission is to pierce through all the encrustations and share direct contact with Jesus. Stott says that the central message of the Gospel is not the teachings of Jesus, but Jesus himself the human/divine figure. He is always bringing people back to the concrete reality of Jesus' life and sacrifice.[1]

It's a compelling reminder that our primary task is not to preach for Christ, or preach about Christ, but to faithfully, simply preach Christ.

'Christ Crucified'

That Christ we preach is more than sage,
more than teacher,
more than reformer,

[1] David Brooks, *The Second Mountain: The Quest for a Moral Life* (New York: Random House Publishing, 2019), 227.

But Christ crucified, an image wrapped in contradiction.

For Paul, the Cross challenges his audience and is the bone all of his hearers choked on. He claims, "Jews demand signs and Greeks look for wisdom, but we preach Christ crucified: a stumbling block to Jews and foolishness to Gentiles, but to those whom God has called, both Jews and Greeks, Christ the power of God and the wisdom of God" (1 Cor. 1:22–24).

The muscular Christianity of the West often starts with Christ as wisdom, a basic "better living through Jesus" approach. It's a compelling sell for an upwardly mobile, middle class audience. But according to Paul, it's not honest. For him, the Cross is an affront to our modern, pain-avoiding, control-seeking, efficiency pursuing sensibilities. A Christ crucified is vulnerable and exposed, a state most of us are scrambling to dodge.

The Cross seems circuitous. Wouldn't a full-frontal assault on evil and darkness win more converts? Weren't there more appealing routes to redeem humanity? Christ crucified is a dangerous starting point for preaching.

It confirms Christ's call for all who would follow him to be symbolically (and for some, literally) crucified. But it's only when God draws people to hold the beauty and the mystery of the Cross that this Christ crucified is unveiled as the power and wisdom of almighty God.

'Peace'

In Ephesians 2, Paul writes, "[Jesus] came and preached peace to you who were far away and peace to those who were near. For through him we both have access to the Father by one Spirit" (vv. 17–18). Some of Jesus' early listeners weren't looking for preaching on peace between rival groups; they were clamoring for victory, vengeance, and vindication.

But Jesus came to preach peace, not just between God and a broken humanity, and not just between one broken individual and another, but between entire tribes, groups, and nations. Christ comes to preach peace to those who are near (like those who have a foundational understanding of Scripture, like a first-century Jewish audience in Palestine) and those who are far (like a Gentile, pagan audience in Asia Minor).

To preach at all means preaching reconciliation in all three dimensions: spiritual, interpersonal, and societal. This peace, this wholeness, this healing is at the core of gospel proclamation. If Jesus comes preaching peace to all groups and among all groups, then it's our responsibility and privilege to follow his lead.

'Anything Helpful'

When Paul said his last goodbye to the Ephesian elders, he said, "You know that I have not hesitated to preach anything that would be helpful to you but have taught you publicly and from house to house" (Acts 20:20). Paul is clear about this central preaching value: Whether he's speaking in formal contexts to crowds or informal contexts to friends, he wants his preaching to be helpful. Other translations of the word here include *profitable, good,* and *expedient.* Paul built such great credibility with his audience that, if he opened his mouth to speak at all, his audience knew his insight would add value to their lives.

As preachers, it's possible to say something accurate, logical, witty, and sound but say it in a manner that's not helpful. Paul's code: If it's helpful, preach it. If it's not, leave it out.

Scripture doesn't just offer insights on what to preach and how to preach it—it explains what happens when effective preaching connects with a specific community in a particular context. Ezra 6:14 says, "So the elders of the Jews continued to build and prosper under the preaching of Haggai the prophet and Zechariah, a descendant of Iddo." Haggai and Zechariah's preaching mobilizes the elders to complete the construction projects they have undertaken. Their words and tone compel their hearers to do the work God is calling them to do. But their words also allow them to flourish in this season of their lives and Israel's history. When we preach well, people aren't just moved. They prosper. And that's my prayer, that as we reclaim a rich tradition of preaching, the people who put themselves under our preaching would thrive.

Our Preaching Audience

'In'

The New Testament includes a few references to places and moments in which preaching occurs.

> "In those days John the Baptist came, preaching in the wilderness of Judea." (Matt. 3:1)

John has a home base for his preaching, and it's not easily accessible. He's preaching in the wilderness because:

- Isaiah said he would;
- He is in the proximity to the Jordan in which to baptize respondents; and
- He's centrally located for people to travel from Jerusalem, Judea, and the broader region.

God places preachers in places at specific times for tactical reasons. John's pulpit was the wilderness, and after his conversation, Paul's place was the synagogues.

If your goal is to baptize, preach near a river.

If your goal is to convince your fellow Jews that Jesus is the Christ, preach where they worship.

> "At once he (Paul) began to preach in the synagogues that Jesus is the Son of God." (Acts 9:20)

Where are you preaching these days? Based on where you are, what is it God is prompting you to say? Are there specific themes that are unique to your location you should be leaning into?

"Preaching in" isn't limited to location, it's also influenced by seasons. Paul tells Timothy, "Preach the word; be prepared in season and out of season; correct, rebuke and encourage—with great patience and careful instruction" (2 Tim. 4:2). If you have the privilege of preaching to the same community over time, you know there are some moments for correction because we're prone to confusion. There are others that demand rebuke because we're tempted to harden our hearts. There are some that call for encouragement because life is hard and we're sometimes tempted to despair. "Preaching in" means being true to the place and the moment that we're in. Jim Elliot said, "Wherever you are, be all there! Live to the hilt every situation you believe to be the will of God." Let it be true of your preaching.

'There'

John the Baptist never left the wilderness to preach, but Jesus didn't wait for people to come to him.

> "Jesus replied, 'Let us go somewhere else—to the nearby villages—so I can preach there also. That is why I have come.' " (Mark 1:38)

I remember my friend Alex McManus told me Jesus' strategy (to preach "there") is counterintuitive for most of us. If you had the success Jesus had in Capernaum, complete with a dramatic public exorcism on your first day of synagogue preaching followed by a litany of healing miracles, would you look to get out of town?

Modern business sense dictates to sell where your customers are, and to put it bluntly, Capernaum was a hot market. It seems like it would be smart for Jesus to build infrastructure for a national teaching and healing ministry in Capernaum and just wait for people to come to him. But he doesn't. Why? Because he didn't come to be a star. He came to go to the region.

Sometimes our desire is to preach "here." We know the people and we like them and they like us. Our kids are settled in their schools. We love our small group and our circle of friends. But if Jesus was ready to preach "there," we have to be ready to preach in places other than the ones we're in. It's not always convenient or easy, but the preacher comes to bring the message to the people, not to get the people to come to him or her.

'To'

Preaching has a where (*here, in, there*) and a who. Jesus told us to go to all nations.

> "And the gospel must first be preached to all nations."
> (Mark 13:10)

I used to think "nations" meant countries, but the word here *ethnos,* is where we get the word *ethnic* or *ethnicities*. The "who" for our preaching is to cover not just language groups or national identities, but subgroups, tribes, and subcultures. This means it's critical for the preacher to understand what it means to contextualize the gospel for a given community or city. It's imperative to understand what makes a different *ethnos* unique and to understand what all people groups have in common.

'Among'

Typically, preachers say they preach "to" a crowd. Sometimes a person will explain he or she felt preached "at." Paul, though, tells his Gentile friends he was able to preach "among" them.

To the Corinthians, he writes, "For the Son of God, Jesus Christ, who was preached among you by us—by me and Silas and Timothy—was not 'Yes' and 'No,' but in him it has always been 'Yes' " (2 Cor. 1:19).

To the Galatians, he explains, "I went in response to a revelation and, meeting privately with those esteemed as leaders, I presented to them the gospel that I preach among the Gentiles" (Gal. 2:2).

For Paul, the Gentiles are family, friends, co-laborers. When he preaches to them, even though they differ from him in ethnicity, spiritual heritage, and worldview, he preaches as one of them. He doesn't demean or patronize the Gentiles; he embraces them. Paul publicly confronts Peter for failing to self-identify as one who is "among" the Gentiles.

To preach "among" is preaching with humility, integrity, and sensitivity to those who are not "my" tribe.

Our Motive for Preaching

'Voluntarily'

Paul says the preaching act is (sometimes) voluntary. In 1 Corinthians 9:16–17, he writes, "For when I preach the gospel, I cannot boast, since I am compelled to preach. Woe to me if I do not preach the gospel! If I preach voluntarily, I have a reward; if not voluntarily, I am simply discharging the trust committed to me."

Paul's declaration that he feels compelled to preach, that he can't imagine not preaching, echoes Jeremiah's exasperation: "His word is in my heart like a fire, a fire shut up in my bones. I am weary of holding it in; indeed, I cannot" (Jer. 20:9).

There are days when we preach because we want to. The words flow freely, the passion is authentic, and our command of the text and the room comes easily. Then there are the other days—when we feel overwhelmed by life, inadequate for the task, and drained by the call. These are the days when, per Jeremiah, it's easier to surrender and let the message out rather than bottle it up. These are the days when, for Paul, we're simply discharging the beautiful and precious trust committed to us.

The more we preach, the more we recognize there are seasons of plenty and seasons of want. But we preach, not because it's always life giving, energizing, or easy, but because we hold, whether confidently or tenuously, something that must be given away.

2

The Preacher As Son/Daughter

When I was in elementary school, my parents volunteered to be the leaders of our local 4-H club. In rural areas, 4-H is well-known for teaching young people to raise livestock. But because I grew up in suburban Chicago, we learned skills like photography, baking, sewing, small-engine repair, and public speaking. My parents encouraged me to enter the public speaking contests. They showed me how to structure, memorize, and deliver a five-minute speech.

When I got up to speak, I always tried to make eye contact with whoever was judging the event. He or she usually had a clipboard with an evaluation sheet. The judges looked for poise, appropriate gestures, dynamics, and clarity of thought; they awarded contestants with a letter grade (A, B, C) and a corresponding ribbon (blue, red, white).

If you won first place at county, you could advance to the state level and give your speech to another group of judges at the state fair. This was another junior speaking society competition with its own rules, rivalries, and incentives. People on the circuit expected and celebrated excellent performances. If you could impress the judges, you would win the day.

When I started high school, one of my teachers encouraged me to join the National Forensic League (now known as the National Speech & Debate Association). In this format, students would draft mock political bills and then debate them in "chamber" at various competitions. Again, adult judges scored the speeches. Students with great speeches would score points for their team; a string of winning speeches won individual trophies and team victories.

But there was another way to win points. If, over the course of the day, you repeatedly won over the room, you could be voted "Best Speaker" by your peers. It was possible to give a speech that failed to impress the judges and still evoke laughs and respect from your colleagues. In some events it was more strategic to give a speech that made you likable rather than one that was technically sound.

I spent a decade in my formative years learning to speak for judges. When I first started preaching regularly, it was difficult to unlearn some of those habits. The most dangerous threat to preachers is seeking identity in their performance as a speaker. When we look to the audience for accolades and affirmation, we don't serve the church well.

We all bring our insecurities into the pulpit with us when we preach, and we can only preach to the edge of those insecurities. When we need the congregation to affirm our worth, we're demanding something they can't deliver. And when they don't give what they're incapable of giving, it only breeds more self-doubt.

The challenge, I'm learning, is to root my identity in relationship to Christ, rather than in the role of preacher. Preaching is what I do; a beloved son is who I am. I can affirm this on a cognitive level without reservation; it's a theologically sound proposition. Nevertheless, I struggle to embrace it on an emotional level. I fail to embody it on a psychological level. It bears repeating because it's easy to forget. To choose it, we have to hear it and receive it, over and over again.

Branding Myself

I have a confession to make. I've heard a few thousand sermons, but I can only remember a few in their entirety. Here's one significant sermon I recall.

It's a crisp October day. I'm a freshman at Taylor University sitting in a packed auditorium for one of our three weekly chapel services. The guest speaker is preaching about the relentless love of God. He said, "When you know you are loved by God, you can live your life with nothing to hide, nothing to prove, and nothing to lose."

I think the reason his message resonated with me so strongly is that when it came to my identity, I was flailing. I was less than two months into this unfamiliar territory. In high school, I knew my place. I knew where to eat lunch. I had a good circle of friends. I was an athlete on the swim team, a member of the speech team, a decent student, an active participant in youth group.

Now, 200 miles away in college, nobody knew my class rank in high school. And nobody cared. I felt compelled to brand myself in those early weeks of college. Maybe I would be the funny guy. Or if I signed up for high-level courses, I could be the campus intellectual. Or if I picked the right flannel shirt and dusted off my barely played guitar, I could be an artist. Or if I joined the campus radio station as a DJ, I could use music and commentary to be a pop culture expert/critic. Or if I joined the traveling drama team, I could be a creative evangelist. Yes, it's a long list. Yes, I experimented with all of these roles.

Then I was sitting in chapel that October day, and it struck me. I was spending an exorbitant amount of time, energy, and psychological bandwidth living with something to prove. My deep-seated insecurities pushed me to convince others I was:

witty,
attractive,
spiritual,
hilarious,
profound,
talented,
significant.

It was exhausting. But if I wasn't loved unconditionally, it was up to me to declare myself worthy to anyone within earshot.

If we're not convinced of our primary identity as beloved sons and daughters, we roll through the wasteland like tumbleweeds, tossed by the whims of others' opinions of us. It's a brutal way to try to live. But to know that we're loved, said the chapel speaker that day, frees us to live (and preach) without shame, self-promotion, or self-protection.

Jesus Was Grounded in His Identity

This is precisely how Jesus operated. He was so grounded in his identity, as framed by his relationship to the Father, that he never stepped outside of it. His teaching never veers towards pettiness, self-focus, or self-doubt. The messenger and the message are a mature, cohesive whole. The Word that was with God declares the words of God in a manner that is unflinching and true. I sometimes ask: How did Jesus get there? How did he evade the temptation to recast his identity based on his personal needs, the whims of the crowds, or the threats of his enemies?

The answer, I believe, lies at Jesus' baptism, the prelude to his public ministry. There are some great sermons (E. V. Hill's "How to Make the Enemy Run") and books (Henri Nouwen's *In the Name of Jesus*) on Christ's baptism and subsequent time in the wilderness.

But my friend Jamie Winship pointed out something I hadn't noticed before in Matthew 3–4.

Winship frames the Devil's temptations as a direct assault on Jesus' identity. Matthew 3:17 says, "And a voice from heaven said, 'This is my Son, whom I love; with him I am well pleased.' " God the Father has publicly and undeniably affirmed Jesus' "beloved Sonness." Just as the Serpent sows doubt about God's trustworthiness to Adam and Eve in Genesis 3 ("Did God really say . . . ?"), the Evil One actively seeks to undercut Jesus' understanding of himself as a beloved son.

The Devil's first challenge begins, "If you are the Son of God, tell these stones to become bread" (Matt. 4:1). He doesn't say, "If you're hungry, tell these stones"; he says, "If you're the Son." Jesus is now forced with a choice. Does he still believe himself to be the Son? He does. And he responds accordingly. He quotes Deuteronomy 8:3. It's interesting to note that Deuteronomy 8:5 says, "Know then in your heart that as a man disciplines his son, so the Lord your God disciplines you." One could argue Jesus is responding with a passage that reaffirms his sonship, not just to the Tempter, but to himself.

The Enemy, undaunted, doubles down. " 'If you are the Son of God,' he said, 'throw yourself down' " (Matt. 4:6). Again, Jesus has to decide. Does he still believe he's the Son? Yes. Now he can respond with confidence: "It is also written: 'Do not put the Lord your God to the test' " (v. 7).

In the third exchange, "The devil took him to a very high mountain and showed him all the kingdoms of the world and their splendor. 'All this I will give you,' he said, 'if you will bow down and worship me' " (vv. 8–9). In a roundabout way, the Devil seems to be poking at Jesus' identity again. The question is: If you're a son to the Father, why are you relegated to a mission to a resistant people in an insignificant corner of the earth? If you're the Son, you deserve more—why don't you take what's yours?" When Jesus defies the Tempter a third time, the Devil finally walks away.

It's only after Jesus firmly anchors his identity that he begins to preach. After his time in the wilderness, Jesus briefly returns to Nazareth and then immediately begins his public ministry in Capernaum. Matthew 4:17 says, "From that time on Jesus began to preach, 'Repent, for the kingdom of heaven has come near.' "

Clarity in Your Identity

Clarity in identity brings freedom in preaching. When we know that we're beloved sons and daughters, we can proclaim truth boldly, choosing to bypass our fears of what others think and confidently give a gift every time we open the text.

When we question our status as beloved sons and daughters, we're prone to preach from a scarcity mentality. There's a limited amount of praise, a limited amount of attention, and a limited amount of applause in the world. As a result, we have to scratch and claw to win it.

I remember preaching on Luke 15 about a father, a runaway son, and a self-righteous big brother. When the younger son finally acknowledges his foolishness and comes home, the father throws an epic party. The older son is openly hostile; he complains that even though he's been a dutiful son, always coloring inside the lines and obeying every rule, Dad never gave him a party.

He says, "Look! All these years I've been slaving for you and never disobeyed your orders. Yet you never gave me even a young goat so I could celebrate with my friends" (Luke 15:29). Look at the verbiage here. The son doesn't define their relationship as father-son but as master-slave. The father responds, "My son . . . you are always with me, and everything I have is yours" (v. 31).

If I'm not the beloved daughter or son, I'm on my own and all I'll ever get is what I win or earn. If, however, I'm a fully loved daughter or son, I can live (and preach) knowing the Father is with me and that I have access to all the Father has. Jesus didn't need to worship the Devil to get glory, splendor, and cities. He already had them; it just wasn't the right season of his life and ministry to use them.

Preachers who view themselves as sons and daughters will still experience pressure, fear, and anxiety at times. They're just not bound by them. They can give themselves away in the pulpit because they know who they are before they think about what they do. They're not conflating their role (preacher) with their identity (beloved child). As a result, they can deliver uncompromising truth to unaccommodating audiences.

Being Secure in Your Identity

The temptation for insecure preachers is to preach to the desires of their pews. Our fears will entice us to dilute the gospel to soothe itching ears. There's an intriguing passage in 1 Kings 22 that compares two kinds of preachers: Zedekiah and Micaiah.

At this point in Israel's history, the people are split into two kingdoms. Ahab is the king of Israel, and Jehoshaphat is the king of Judah. Ahab decides he's ready to attack Ramoth Gilead, a historic Israelite city occupied by Arameans, their enemy to the east. There hasn't been any conflict between the two armies for three years. Ahab, however, is itching for a fight and invites Jehoshaphat to join him.

Jehoshaphat agrees to partner with Ahab on one condition: that they seek the counsel of the Lord together. So Ahab convenes about 400 male prophets and asks them, "Shall I go to war against Ramoth Gilead, or shall I refrain?" In unison they reply, "Go . . . for the Lord will give it into the king's hand" (v. 6). But the king of Judah is wary. He asks Ahab a telling question, "Is there no longer a prophet of the Lord here whom we can inquire of?" (v. 7). Jehoshaphat is a discerning audience; he would rather hear the simple truth from one preacher than a lie proclaimed by a chorus of hundreds.

Ahab flinches. "There is still one prophet through whom we can inquire of the Lord, but I hate him because he never prophesies anything good about me, but always bad. He is Micaiah son of Imlah" (v. 8). Ahab's posture directly contradicts Jehoshaphat's.

Ahab will gladly entertain mistruths and half-truths as long as they paint him in a positive light. In the words of Paul, Ahab is the personification of those who, in an attempt to "suit their own desires," surround themselves with teachers "to say what their itching ears want to hear" (2 Tim. 4:3).

Nevertheless, at Jehoshaphat's urging, Ahab summons Micaiah. While the kings wait, Ahab's prophets are promising him success for his scheme. Some of these prophets go out of their way to stand out from their peers. One, Zedekiah, made iron horns and, posing with them, dramatically declares that these are words from God, "With these you will gore the Arameans until they are destroyed" (1 Kings 22:11). If Ahab is looking for a prophet who will tell him what he longs to hear, he has one in Zedekiah.

The official who escorts Micaiah to the kings' thrones advises, "Look, the other prophets without exception are predicting success for the king. Let your word agree with theirs, and speak favorably" (v. 13). But Micaiah is steadfast. After initially, and maybe sarcastically, toeing the party line, Micaiah explains the attack will fail. When pressed on why his message is a stark departure from the rest of the group, Micaiah says it's because a deceiving spirit has influenced the prophets' words in order to lead Ahab to his death (v. 23).

Zedekiah is so incensed he physically assaults and publicly insults Micaiah, slapping him in the face. Zedekiah asks, "Which way did the spirit from the Lord go when he went from me to speak to you?" (v. 24). Micaiah responds, "You will find out on the day you go to hide in an inner room" (v. 25). The crowd is stunned. The messages are polar opposites. Someone is lying. But only Micaiah has a proven track record for speaking words of truth.

Ahab, however, attacks Ramoth Gilead anyway. Per Micaiah's prophecy, he dies. And Jehoshaphat barely escapes with his life.

Zedekiah and Micaiah offer a unique case study on identity and preaching.

Who put more time and energy into impressing the high-profile audience here? The writer of 2 Kings tells us Zedekiah "made iron horns." Zedekiah is a career prophet. He's not a metalworker or a blacksmith. Consider the time, effort, and cost Zedekiah put into his preaching prop. If "all the prophets" are speaking before the kings of Judah and Israel, Zedekiah needs to do something noteworthy to stand out. He certainly does.

Imagine the drama, the spectacle of Zedekiah doing his best impersonation of a bull dramatically goring a group of imaginary Arameans to their deaths. If this is a prophesying contest, Zedekiah is the clear winner. Zedekiah is preaching with something to prove. He's bold, innovative, and comes with a message everyone wants to hear.

Then there's Micaiah. He's not a part of the fanfare or the group-think. Micaiah doesn't have time or energy for the charade at the threshing floor. The messenger likely perceives Micaiah is a reluctant participant and offers some notes for his sermon. "You don't even have to prepare a poetic talk this time. Just declare success for the king like everyone else. There's a great spread in the green room and you'll get a nice honorarium. Don't overthink this one."

At first glance, Micaiah appears to fold. He parrots the party line about victory and glory for Ahab and Jehoshaphat. Ahab, however, knows better. Apparently, he and Micaiah have done this dance enough times for everyone to know how it ends. Maybe Micaiah utters his initial "prophecy" with a smirk, a scowl, or the sarcasm his contemporary Elijah uses at Mount Carmel.

Eventually, Micaiah relents and preaches what he knows to be true, unpopular as it is: "I saw all Israel scattered on the hills like sheep without a shepherd, and the Lord said, 'These people have no master. Let each one go home in peace' " (1 Kings 22:17). Micaiah isn't just saying something unfavorable; his message undermines the legitimacy of Ahab's monarchy and questions the credibility of all the other prophets present.

Zedekiah's not an idiot. He knows Micaiah's message might ruin his moment. He's so flustered he slaps Micaiah and asks, How do we know you heard from God? Micaiah responds with the ultimate knockout comeback: Because I spend time alone in a room communing with God. And you don't.

Zedekiah's message was born out of his need for approval and affirmation. Make no mistake, it was a powerful presentation. Given the techniques of his time, it was well-executed. And all wrong.

Micaiah's delivery was anticlimactic. He didn't have a prop or great lighting or stirring images on a screen. He just had the simple message that came directly out of his regular, private conversations with God. Micaiah knows who he is and to whom he belongs. He'll risk rejection, humiliation, financial hardship, even death. He's got nothing to hide, nothing to prove, and nothing to lose.

Ahab sends Micaiah to prison, restricting him to a diet of bread and water until he returns. Micaiah answers, "If you ever return safely, the Lord has not spoken through me" (1 Kings 22:28). Ahab dies in the ensuing battle, and we never hear how Micaiah's story ends.

Start with Your Identity in Christ, then Move to Your Message

Charles de Gaulle, the leader of post–World War II France, always tried to say what people expected him to say when he spoke. I can understand how that might generate longevity for a politician, but it's poison for the preacher. Rather than starting with one's identity and moving toward the message, his model started with appeasing the audience and worked backwards toward content.

If our identity is shaky, every message is a performance. If our identity is grounded, every sermon is a gift. In his book *A Life in Parts,* award-winning actor Bryan Cranston describes a formative shift in how he viewed auditioning for parts. Early in his career, he came to auditions feeling anxious. The goal was to win the part. Every line, gesture, and movement was done for the casting director's approval. Later, Cranston decided to view the process differently. Rather than "pitching" himself, he committed to getting lost in the role. He fully invested himself in the lines, out of love for the craft and commitment to the character, because his intent wasn't to win the role but to give a gift to those who saw him embody the role.

The best gifts are given without expecting anything in return. When we preach as beloved sons and daughters, we preach with such great love for our people that we refuse to demand anything from them: not applause, not glory, not wealth. Why? Because the Father reminds us, "You are always with me and everything I have is yours."

When we don't crave accolades, it's easy to pass them along when they do come. I heard Corrie ten Boom say that when she got compliments, she would graciously receive them and make a mental note. Then, at the end of the day, she presented them like an invisible bouquet of flowers to her Father in heaven, praying, "These belong to you."

Yes, we can only preach to the edge to our insecurities. But when we ground ourselves in our identity as beloved sons and daughters, those insecurities fade into the periphery. We can preach like we have nothing to prove and nothing to lose, because we don't. Not anymore.

So preach like he is always with you and everything he has is yours.

3

The Preacher As Listener

When I was a child, I noticed one Sunday ritual that would take place every week. When Pastor Bob got up to preach, my mom pulled a pen and a small notebook from her purse to take sermon notes. When I was in middle school, I followed her lead. Recently my wife, Kelly, and I were cleaning out our basement, and I found a box of spiral notebooks with sermons notes from 20 years ago. There were notes from church services, church conferences, and even churches we visited on vacation. The date, the pastor, the location, and the sermon title are at the top of each page. Mom said you listen better if you write your thoughts down as you hear them; I think she's right.

I once heard an author say that when writers write, they give you a gift—not just their wisdom, but their time. The same is true for preachers. When the preacher opens their mouth, they're giving you their time spent in prayer, in study, in reflection, in community with those they serve. In a way, the preacher functions as an indirect spiritual mentor to the congregation. And our own preaching is formed, both consciously and unconsciously, by the preachers we've heard.

Over the past 30 years, only a handful of people have actively mentored me in my preaching. But dozens of preachers, some whose names I've forgotten, in churches I've attended physically and virtually, domestically and globally, have influenced me through their sermons. Here's a few of the lessons they taught me.

A Preacher's Perspective

At the most fundamental level, preachers with more experience and training offer insights into the text the listener doesn't have. I remember a recording of Tim Keller preaching the story of Joseph from Genesis 39–40. Keller identified three temptations Joseph faced in his ordeal. The obvious temptation was to pursue a sexual encounter with Potiphar's wife. The less obvious temptation was to abuse his power for personal gain. Keller caught me by surprise, though, when he said Joseph's most dangerous temptation was the temptation to despair. I'd never stopped to consider Joseph's fragile emotional state while locked in Pharaoh's dungeon.

Keller preached a text I knew. And yet, like a fine jeweler holding a diamond up to the light, he turned that text to refract colors and tones I didn't know were there.

A Preacher's Social Location

In my early 30s, after serving as a youth pastor, associate pastor, and church planter, I returned to southern California for a graduate school seminar. One evening, when I was tired of thinking and writing, I took a break to explore a new program the school was offering to develop and form preachers. The initiative was called Micah Groups, a cohort-based, yearlong journey to help preachers of different ethnicities, genders, and denominational backgrounds address the intersection of worship, preaching, and justice.

The project was created by Mark Labberton, who, in addition to leading First Presbyterian Church of Berkeley, was also leading the Lloyd John Ogilvie Institute of Preaching at Fuller Theological

Seminary. Mark was the first person I heard explain the impact of a preacher's social location on his or her preaching. Not long after he introduced this concept to me, I wrote an introductory chapter for an academic project that included a section on "limitations." To give the reader context for my point of view, I needed to clearly identify what personal, geographic, and ideological issues potentially hindered the objectivity of my research.

While I have often been told that our background and life experience is an asset to our preaching, it is also a liability. I don't have to feel shame for my limitations, but I must acknowledge them. Our social location includes race, gender, marital status, family of origin, education, nationality, church background, ministry experience, and geography.

A failure to accurately name my social location blinds me to the limits of my preaching. However, when I see and acknowledge those limits, I can admit my need to hear from voices that aren't limited in the same way mine is.

One of the amazing women I met through the Micah Groups was Sara Barton, chaplain of Pepperdine University. In one of our conversations, we discussed how our social location influences our reading of a given text. Sara explained how she read the story of David and Bathsheba with a group of women in Uganda. Their initial response was "Bathsheba was raped!" Their perspective on the power dynamics in the story told them Bathsheba was not a willing party to her encounter with David. Their unique vantage point as women and Ugandans allowed Sara to see a dimension in the narrative she hadn't previously seen.

The beauty of globalization is that we are hearing from voices we wouldn't have otherwise heard. Over the course of my studies in missiology, I traveled to Israel and Palestine a number of times. I met courageous people like Baruch Maoz, a Jewish-Israeli follower of Jesus, whose preaching profoundly shaped my understanding of unity, reconciliation, and contextualization. I connected with Arab-Israeli Palestinian Christians Jack Sara and Salim Munayer, who taught me similar themes from their own unique perspective. All three of these preachers preached not just with their words, but with their lives, modeling and declaring *shalom* in the midst of a conflict zone. When I have the opportunity to speak about the gospel's power to bridge cultural and political divides, I seek input from these mentors.

These mentor-teacher-preachers are an ever-growing cloud of witnesses that transcend race, gender, denominational affiliation, and theological distinctive. They are singing like a hallowed chorus, reminding me that:

- The truths we proclaim are both simple and rich,
- The contexts in which we declare them are both beautiful and broken,
- The hearts from which we preach are scarred yet leaning toward wholeness,
- Our voices can be bold and clear or cracking and hoarse, and
- The task, while noble, is not always easy.

They help me to faithfully lift up a compelling portrait of Christ and his kingdom.

A Preacher's Unique Style

Billy Graham's preaching plays a unique role in my family story. When my father was a student at Stanford University, he heard Graham speak at a chapel service. He preached on the worth of a human life. My dad remembered him listing the commercial value of the elements that comprise a human body. At that time, the going rate for the correct amount of oxygen, carbon, hydrogen, nitrogen, calcium, and phosphorus was about $2.50. Graham went on to declare that a human life is worth more than the sum of its components, that Christ went to the Cross because every life matters to God.

Graham mastered the ability to connect with audiences across the socioeconomic and educational spectrum. He was relentless in his attempts to frame the gospel in simple, easy-to-understand terms. As an anthropologist, he believed in connecting his message of hope to four transcendent human struggles: loneliness, emptiness, guilt, and the fear of death. He strove to connect with people at a gut level, meeting them at their point of need. Every time I get ready to preach a message, I ask, "Emotionally and psychologically, where are the people I'll be preaching to? What is their fundamental need? What are their key questions?"

Graham reminds me that a preacher's style emerges from their unique personality. He captured the essence of "preacher." His passion was undeniable, his character unassailable, and his conviction unmovable. In his 1991 biography, *A Prophet with Honor,* William Martin notes that Graham, as a young man,

> poured every possible ounce of his talent and commitment into his preaching. . . . His exuberant gestures and high-speed delivery won him the nickname the Preaching Windmill, and nearly everyone who heard him mentioned the uncommon amount of noise he could generate in the pulpit.[1]

---

[1] William Martin, *A Prophet with Honor: The Billy Graham Story* (New York: William Morrow, 1991), 77.

Graham's legacy says I can communicate the complex without confusing a congregation. Inserting perplexing words, phrases, names, or stories into sermons isn't reflective of our intelligence. If anything, it betrays our arrogance and insecurity. Yes, sometimes it's harder to distill important truths into understandable verbiage, but both the text and the hearer deserve our best effort.

A Preacher's Core Themes

A friend once told me, "Every preacher only has two or three main sermons. They just repackage them differently." If you have a favorite preacher, my guess is you could easily distill their primary themes down to a short list.

John the Baptist continually called people to repent and display behavior reflecting their alignment with God's righteousness. Ezekiel's catchphrase could be "Then they will know that I am the Lord." All preachers have a go-to text, a motif they revisit because it's hardwired into their spiritual DNA.

I recall two themes in two speakers that have influenced my preaching: loving God with my mind and immersing myself in the emotional tension of the text.

One preacher is Jay Kesler, the president of Taylor University when I was a student. Kesler modeled the practice of constant curiosity. He repeatedly challenged the false dichotomy between faith and reason and urged us to love God with all our minds. As a university president he championed the value of the academic disciplines. In one chapel service he said that in our pursuit of knowledge, "we don't have to be afraid that something's going to jump out from underneath a rock and eat God. And if it does, we'll just have to worship that instead." Kesler was convinced that intellectual questions served, rather than threatened, our spiritual formation.

He was always reading, always learning, and regularly watched one hour of MTV a week in order to keep his finger on the pulse of youth culture. His commitment to learning and research gave him credibility with a wide number of audiences, but his humility and grace disarmed people who were inclined to disagree with his worldview.

The second preacher is Erwin McManus. I first heard McManus speak at an evangelism conference in my late 20s. McManus isn't just a student of culture; he's committed to shaping it. Much of the preaching I'd heard in my previous circles was a call to avoid, resist, or copy the themes or modes of popular culture. Erwin's view of God as creator and life-giver compels me to see myself and the church as co-creators with God.

If God spoke the universe into existence and we partner with God in the creative endeavor, McManus says, "What is God currently speaking to us? And what does he want to speak through us?"

I heard McManus speak again when I was taking graduate courses near Los Angeles. He asked, "Have you ever thought of the questions you'd ask God if you had the chance to meet him face to face?" He paused long enough for us to allow those questions to surface. He gave some examples:

> "Where were you when . . . ?"
> "Why did you allow . . . ?"
> "How come you never . . . ?"

He then continued, "Have you ever stopped to consider God might have questions for you?" He then launched into the list of questions God posed to Adam and Eve in Genesis 3:

> "Where are you?"
> "Who told you that you were naked?"

> "Have you eaten from the tree I commanded you not to eat from?"
> "What is this you have done?"

For me, McManus mastered the art of immersing the audience in the emotional tension of a text. He modeled the power of using questions to open a dialogue not just between the listener and the preacher, but directly with God.

I never saw McManus speak with a full manuscript. When we eventually had a chance to meet in person, he explained he would sometimes put a short note inside his Bible with a broad outline for his talk. He told me, "If you have to read what you believe, people may question whether or not it's really in you." It's a challenge I've carried with me ever since. If I have to choose between great phrasing or being fully present with an audience, I want to opt for being present—mentally, visually, spiritually.

McManus taught me to approach the text and the preaching moment with anticipation, wonder, and assertiveness. He helped me dismantle a flawed construct about evangelistic preaching versus discipleship-based preaching. In one instance, when asked how he preached when both Christians and non-Christians are present, he simply replied "I just speak to humans." His anthropology is not dissimilar to Billy Graham's. There are issues that are common to people at various stages of their spiritual journey. Speak to those and you'll connect with people across the spectrum.

These two voices have indirectly mentored me through their insights on the text, their own social locations, their stories, their personalities, and their personal histories.

A Preacher's Mentoring

My story would be incomplete without mentioning Phil Collins, who mentored me for two years, and Ken Davis, who has shaped my preaching over two decades. Phil was the adjunct professor in my college courses on student ministry. For reasons that still aren't entirely clear to me, Phil invited me to speak to his youth group in suburban Indianapolis. And not just once—he entrusted me with all of the preaching for a retreat with his high school students. I believe we discussed themes and content, but Phil never dictated how I should preach. The invitation was a blessing and an investment. Sure, Phil had invested in me in the classroom, but here he fully empowered me, to declare the gospel to his students.

Since that moment, I've tried to give emerging preachers opportunities that will affirm and stretch them. I understand different traditions have specific requirements about who can preach and where and when they can do so. My prayer is that you can be creative about how to find space to encourage and elevate new voices who are called and committed to preaching.

If Phil's mentoring was passive, Ken Davis is active. I heard Ken speak when I was a freshman in college and a few years later took his workshop on the basics of communication. Over the next several years, I took his advanced course and volunteered to help with his basic class. Ken took issue with a statement about preaching: "That person makes the Bible come alive." I believe he said, "The Bible isn't dead. We just keep killing it."

Twenty years after meeting Ken, I realized I'd hit a wall in my preaching. I was still energized by the idea of preaching and cherished every chance to lift up the text before spiritually hungry people, but I knew my preaching was stuck. So, with encouragement from the head of our church staff, I reached out to Ken to see if he would listen to two messages of mine a year and give me feedback. Ken graciously agreed. And over the past two years, he's given me invaluable feedback that I couldn't get from family, colleagues, or congregants.

Proverbs 27:6 says, "Wounds from a friend can be trusted, but an enemy multiplies kisses." The people who love us aren't our adversaries, but generic encouragement is the enemy of excellent preaching. I needed Davis, an objective outside observer, to remind me that the rapid tempo in my introductions wasn't engaging people but was distracting them. My attempt to engage everyone with direct eye contact meant that I wasn't really connecting with any part of the room in a meaningful way. And my propensity to speak in metaphors was sabotaging my desire to speak with clarity.

It wasn't all critique. When Ken gave a compliment, I took it to heart; it came from a seasoned, veteran preacher. His encouragement sustained me through a brutal season in which I questioned my call and lost much of my confidence. I am immensely grateful for the gift that he's been to me—my preaching is better because it's been under his microscope.

A Preacher's Attentive Listening

Faithful preaching is born out of attentive listening. Peter listened to Jesus for years. It gave him the framework he needed to speak without formal preparation at Pentecost. Paul listened to the disciples in Damascus before he preached Christ in a synagogue. Later, Timothy listened to Paul. Apollos listened to Aquila and Priscilla. When he did, "he was a great help to those who by grace had believed" (Acts 18:27).

If you're new on your preaching journey, pause to take inventory of the voices that have shaped you and how. If you've got a few hundred sermons under your belt, keep listening. There's always something new to learn, about the text, about the world, and about yourself.

4

The Preacher As Fellow Traveler

I've always been fascinated by historic pulpits, from the Ambon of Henry II in the Aachen Cathedral to John Wesley's traveling pulpit of wood and canvas to Billy Graham's IBM pulpit. But it's the elevated pulpit, the one with a winding staircase, that's always captured my imagination.

I asked my friend Pete van der Harst, who's an engineer and consultant for church auditorium designs, about the advantages of preaching from a perch. He says, in addition to helping the audience see the preacher, the added height allowed congregants in longer, rectangular spaces, to hear the message with greater clarity.

Until the advent and use of the microphone in churches, the raised pulpit served to literally amplify the message. The danger, however, of speaking "from above," is to be disconnected from the daily experiences of the listener. I recently heard a preacher slip the phrase "Augustinian soteriology" into a regular Sunday morning service. The audience smiled and nodded politely, but my guess is that the line went over most of their heads. When we start with theological expertise or the more technical points of doctrine that are foreign to our hearers, we preach from "above." When we moralize, sermonize, or patronize our people, we preach from "above." Even if our intentions are good, our words can sail over, rather than toward, people.

Preaching from 'Among'

Mark Labberton speaks of the importance of preaching "from among" the people rather than "from above." Often congregations expect preachers to know and speak definitive answers for all of life's complex challenges. Preaching as we walk with and alongside the congregation liberates the pastor and empowers the church to navigate the complexities of faith.

In 2 Timothy 4:2, Paul writes, "Preach the word; be prepared in season and out of season; correct, rebuke and encourage—with great patience and careful instruction." While the goal is non-negotiable (correct, rebuke, and encourage), the tone with which we deliver it should flex and bend depending on who we're preaching to. Encouraging a group of lifelong churchgoers in rural West Texas looks different than encouraging a group of new believers in urban Seattle.

Preaching that ignores context is sloppy. It imposes a style or verbiage on the listener rather than pulling him or her in. Paul's instruction to include "great patience" implies patience with the listener, but also patience with the process. "Careful instruction" means we think deliberately about how to connect with hearers in a given place at a particular moment.

The COVID-19 pandemic forced preachers in affected areas to think creatively about how to deliver content without a gathered congregation. Some pastors with the technical resources to do so prerecorded their preaching earlier in the week and then broadcast those services on Sunday. The upside was the ability to offer something with higher production value for the congregants viewing or listening. The downside, of course, is that prerecorded messages don't account for the most recent events that may be on a church's or a city's mind.

In the greater Grand Rapids area, public demonstrations in response to George Floyd's death on Monday, May 25, 2020, reached a flashpoint on Saturday evening (May 30), with a string of vehicles burning on Pearl Street Northwest. The Grand Rapids community was shaken; it was a prime opportunity to speak healing and challenging words in the wake of both national and local turmoil. But some churches in the area didn't address these events at all. They couldn't preach "among" because their prerecorded sermons prevented them from being in the same spiritual, emotional, and psychological space as their people.

When people are struggling, they need to feel like their preacher is in the fire with them. I learned this the hard way when I registered in January for the Detroit marathon a few years ago. The goal was to raise money for clean water initiatives operated by our ministry partners in northern Kenya. I invited anyone from our church who wanted to be a part of our team to run with me.

Then April came and I trained some. May brought a slight uptick in my workouts, but not nearly enough to stay on schedule. Life happened, I got lazy, and by the time race day came in late October, I was officially ill equipped to run a full marathon. I had, however, raised some money for our cause and also roped a good number of people from our church into joining me. At that point, I kind of had to do it.

Two of my sisters graciously made the trip to Detroit from Chicago to help me through the first 13.1 miles. They were a true gift and an amazing help. It wasn't until about mile 17 that the wheels started to come off. My body was aching, and my mind started to unravel.

About that time three women from my church who were wearing shirts for our charity came running by. One said, "Hey Steve. We've brought a verse to read for every mile of the marathon. Want to hear it?"

I was already in a rough spot, and now I was embarrassed that my race strategy was not nearly as spiritual as theirs. Wincing, I nodded. With clarity and confidence, she quoted Isaiah 41:10: "So do not fear, for I am with you; do not be dismayed, for I am your God. I will strengthen you and help you; I will uphold you with my righteous right hand."

My eyes welled up. I had forgotten how true the words she quoted really are. Granted, it was my own dumb fault I was in this mess, but even so I needed to hear God say, "I will strengthen you and help you."

It wasn't the words themselves that mattered in the moment. There were hundreds of spectators cheering generic encouragement and even friends and family members who came to cheer for me by name. But the "sermon" my running friends offered was compelling because they were tired too. Their quads and calves were aching too, and their journey gave credibility to their words, because we were all in it together.

Identify with People

To preach above is to stand outside of people. To preach among is to identify with them, to name their dreams, their hopes, their wrongs, and their rebellion.

Jonah or Jeremiah

This is the difference between Jonah and Jeremiah. Jonah doesn't really want to preach from among. He walks the streets of Nineveh for three days and then promptly leaves town to build a private viewing stand from which to watch the apocalypse. Jonah is preaching from above. His doctrine is right, his heritage is right; but his posture is all wrong. Despite his own shortcomings and recent rebellion, Jonah can't (or won't) identify with the Assyrians. He's done his duty and refuses to be emotionally invested in the lives of the people who are moved by his message.

Now look at Jeremiah. He's been preaching a brutal message of destruction to Jerusalem for years. At God's direction, Jeremiah's preaching includes some vivid object lessons and illustrations. He shatters a jar in the Valley of Ben Hinnom and he buries a linen belt in Perath. When he returns to the temple court of Jerusalem and preaches destruction again, it's too much for Pashhur. He has Jeremiah arrested, beaten, and put in stocks overnight. And all this happens in the shadow of the temple, the house that bears God's name.

The next morning, Pashhur releases Jeremiah. Jeremiah prophesies exile and heartache for Pashhur, punishment for his propensity to prophesy lies. This is the backdrop for Jeremiah's complaint to God. He says, "Whenever I speak, I cry out proclaiming violence and destruction. So the word of the Lord has brought me insult and reproach all day long. But if I say, 'I will not mention his word or speak anymore in his name,' his word is in my heart like a fire, a fire shut up in my bones. I am weary of holding it in; indeed, I cannot" (Jer. 20:8–9).

Jeremiah is exhausted from preaching among. He doesn't have the luxury of telegraphing his missives from afar; these are words that have to land on the temple porch. And Jeremiah must stand among Pashhur and his associates to deliver them.

It's a high-stakes endeavor. Jeremiah's life has already been threatened once. And now he's directly challenging the people with the power to destroy him. His "fire in my bones" speech is a lament for his life and preaching career. But his personal lament is just a sliver of his total work. The broad view of Jeremiah's prophecy is a dirge for the people and the city he loves.

As someone committed to preaching from among, Jeremiah is an embedded prophet. He's not going to hurl sermon points at Judah as he runs away from their impending punishment. He's going to walk with them to the bitter end.

Jesus

Like Jeremiah, Jesus models a "preach among" style. Yes, Jesus preached from the standard pulpit of his day, when he spoke in the synagogues of Capernaum and Nazareth. But the bulk of Jesus' teaching happened informally, in fields and on hills, on roads and in the temple courts, on the beach and in a boat. Mark 4:1–2 says, "Again Jesus began to teach by the lake. The crowd that gathered around him was so large that he got into a boat and sat in it out on the lake, while all the people were along the shore at the water's edge. He taught them many things by parables. . . ."

Jesus' preaching is proximate to where people are, not just physically, but culturally, psychologically, and emotionally. If we intend to follow his model, we must be versed in our community's history and makeup, our congregation's story and legends, and our people's experiences, both the remarkable and the mundane.

Contextualized Preaching

Contextualized preaching requires more than an understanding of broader cultural themes and trends. It demands a solid grasp of a community's history. I believe the preacher should know a city's history and symbols at least as well as the average churchgoer.

When I was a church leader in suburban Detroit, our team realized a significant number of people attending our Sunday evening service were college students from the city. Over time, we started exploring the idea of moving that service to Midtown, the neighborhood where the university is located. We spoke to church members who lived in and near Midtown and researched the history of the city itself.

The imagery in the Detroit city flag continues to capture my imagination. The flag is divided into four quarters. The bottom left has five gold fleurs-de-lis on a white field, a nod to the French who built the first European settlement on the river. The upper right quadrant includes three gold lions on a red field to denote the 36 years the British occupied the fort. The upper left and bottom right depict, respectively, 13 stars and 13 stripes to represent the American colonies. Without any text, the flag portrays three hundred years of history in the city.

But it's the circle in the center that shaped my preaching: an image of loss and hope. This seal represents the aftermath of the fire on June 11, 1805. Historians say a local baker, John Harvey, started a fire in his stables when he knocked some ashes out of his smoking pipe. The blaze leveled the city of mostly wooden structures. Only a stone fort and a few brick chimneys were left in the city of 600 residents. When the smoke cleared, a French priest, Gabriel Richard, wrote the line that would become the city motto, the line portrayed in the center of the flag.

On the left, a woman gestures toward the burning city. The Latin phrase *Speramus Meliora* ("We hope for better things") serves as a caption for this image. On the right, another woman consoles her grieving friend with one hand while pointing to a rebuilt city with the other. The text here reads *Resurget Cineribus* ("It will rise from the ashes.").

Hope and *resurrection* were themes we wanted to reflect in our service and our teaching. One passage that kept coming to mind during this season was Isaiah 58:12: "Your people will rebuild the ancient ruins and will raise up the age-old foundations; you will be called Repairer of Broken Walls, Restorer of Streets with Dwellings."

Ten years later, I realize we may have understood the symbols, but we didn't understand the stories of those who had historic roots in the surrounding neighborhood. Our efforts in Midtown focused on the mostly Anglo, middle-class, college and medical school students in the neighborhood. They were transplants and travelers, and we aimed to reach them. But we were ignorant of the people, the themes, the wisdom, joy, and struggle in the neighborhoods that were just blocks off of Woodward, the newly revitalized thoroughfare with new housing, dining, and shopping.

Understanding a community's history includes learning about a town's current demographics. It's asking, "Who lives here?" and "Why?" A few years ago, my friend James Ellis III gave me *The Warmth of Other Suns*, a book on African American migration from the Jim Crow South to cities like Chicago, New York, and Los Angeles. It's must-read for any preacher doing work in cities with a historic black presence. It paints a picture of the hope people are pushing toward, the yearning to bounce back from the tragedy and injustice, from this generation, not a centuries-old event.

When I was 20, my first full-time church job was as a youth pastor for a five-year-old church plant 10 miles north of the Detroit city limits. I remember taking a tour of the local high school, where our church had services on Sunday, and seeing flags representing students from 80 different countries in the hallway. I learned the automotive industry was bringing engineers, executives, and line workers from all over the world. In the subdivision behind the high school, I heard that it wasn't uncommon for Indian, Korean, Anglo, and African American families to live on the same cul-de-sac.

Understanding Our People

Ultimately, preaching among, is about knowing a people, their history, their present, and their yearnings for a new future.

Preaching among at the mid-level is understanding the context of a particular people or moment. Jesus is constantly drawing themes from the daily lives of his hearers: fish and water, fields and flowers, sheep and shepherds. And Jesus pivots based on who his audience is: He speaks plainly to peasants but is able shift gears to connect with the religious and political elite of his day as well.

Of course, if a speaker doesn't identify with an individual or congregation, the hearers sense it immediately. It's like when the American rock star Bruce Springsteen mistakenly referred to fans at a concert in Cleveland, Ohio, as residents of Pittsburgh, Pennsylvania. Identifying with people means asking questions about their lives and challenges between sermons so we don't make wrong assumptions when we get up to preach those sermons.

In my mid-20s, I took a summer away from student ministry to take my systematic theology courses at graduate school. I had just gotten out of a complicated dating relationship and was intrigued when I saw a posting for free counseling through the seminary's school of psychology. I remember meeting the graduate student in a counseling office and walking him through my recent journey.

At one point, trying to make a personal connection, he said, "Steve, this is kind of like your soccer." I was perplexed. I hadn't played soccer competitively since I was in elementary school. Then I realized he was referring to my T-shirt that, along with the brand's logo, had an image of a soccer ball. It was an honest mistake. Nevertheless, I didn't go back. The grad student thought he knew something about me but never stopped to clarify. To identify with means carving out time for meaningful conversations with church members and hearing what's challenging them and moving them.

Identifying with requires the humility to acknowledge we haven't experienced the breadth of human experience everyone in the audience has. And it requires the tenacity to say, "Help me understand where you've been and where you're going."

Preaching among commits to knowing a community, a church, and the individuals that comprise it. A few years ago, I was preaching on the value of work and vocation. Without fully thinking it through, at the end of one sermon I offered to visit anyone in the church at their place of work over the course of the four-week series. I had this gnawing sense that many hearing the messages I was giving appreciated my sentiment but doubted my ability to fully understand their work environment. The next few weeks were a valuable lesson in listening and learning.

Bill invited me to his egg farm, where he showed me how his company processes its own chicken feed, cares for its birds, and packages eggs. Dave walked me through the massive floor of a frozen-food manufacturing plant, where I witnessed line workers and machines generate 700 frozen lasagnas a minute. Steve explained the complexities of installing new networks and communicators for a system as a part of the IT team for a major local hospital group. Karen gave me tour of a thrift store that receives, processes, and sells donated items to send Bibles to South America. Stephanie asked if I would come to the fast-food restaurant she works for, and when I arrived she was serving customers with a smile. Nate taught me some of the challenges and joys of acting as the senior vice president for design and ideation for a global consumer products company.

The visits I made over those few short weeks were an exercise in walking among. They equipped me to preach among our people, especially on a topic I needed their help to understand.

Walking With

Yes, pastors and preachers walk with church members through milestone moments—weddings, funerals, baptisms, infant dedications, graduations, and the like. These moments matter, but in many cases, they are planned and have an accompanying script. Preaching as a fellow traveler means committing to walk with people in the mundane, ordinary moments that don't require a clergy person to officiate, coordinate, or pontificate.

The former US Secretary of Defense, General Jim Mattis, wrote in his memoir about the value of having direct access to those he was responsible for. He says, "I did not rely on the chain of command to bring all important issues to my attention. I let it be known that every Friday afternoon I would be at the club for happy hour. As one man explained, when asked why Robert Burns wrote his poetry in taverns, it was in those places that one could hear 'the elemental passions, the open heart and the bold tongue, and no masks.'"[1] In this spirit, every preacher should consider holding "open office hours" somewhere in the public square, where they can get a pulse on what is grieving or energizing their people.

Walking with means slowing down, matching the pace of your hearers, even if you feel like you're revisiting ground you've already covered. I remember taking a personality test (CliftonStrengths) a few years ago. One of the trainers at the workshop mentioned how important it is for parents to understand that their children are wired and gifted in ways that are different than them. He said the temptation for most parents is to "minimize" and "project."

When a talent comes naturally for a person, it's difficult for him or her to realize it doesn't come easily to others. They "minimize" their skill because they're either naturally hardwired for it or they have years of experience at it. The next problem is that they "project," they inadvertently communicate to their children: "This is easy for me; it should be easy for you." It's a disempowering posture. Children start to feel overwhelmed and inadequate because they

[1] Jim Mattis and Bing West, *Call Sign Chaos: Learning to Lead* (New York: Random House, 2019), 156–157.

don't have the same gifts as their parents.

If we're not careful, we as preachers can do the same. If we don't commit to walking with people, we can end up running ahead or lagging behind. Rather than permitting hearers to be where they are, we speak to where we think they should be. Instead of declaring peace and joy, we preach pressure and guilt. We end up modeling a "try harder" mentality rather than a "my yoke is easy" mindset.

In the end, we're either walking with our people or we're not. There's no faking it if we aren't and no denying it if we are.

A few years after I planted our church in suburban Detroit, I met Dan and Ronia at one of our services. We immediately connected because their son was just a few months older than our daughter and because Dan is a surgeon and my wife, Kelly, is a nurse.

We were thrilled when we discovered that Ronia and Kelly were both expecting their second child in July of 2004. And we were devastated to learn Ronia's baby, a boy, was diagnosed in utero with trisomy 18, a condition the medical community calls "incompatible with life." Ronia bravely carried the son, who she named Isaac, to term.

I'll never forget getting the call on a Sunday morning right before church that Isaac had been born and that Dan and Ronia were able to hold him for a short while before he passed away. The sermon that Sunday was part of series titled "Yelling at God." I don't remember exactly what I said, but I remember the space I was in. I wasn't preaching to the Dans and Ronias of the world, I was preaching with them, for their story brought the beauty of love and the hope of the resurrection into sharp relief for our church, not just for a day but for the entirety of their time with us.

Preaching among a people is exponentially more challenging than preaching from above them. It involves a willingness to do your homework, to listen with the intent to learn, and to spend time outside of the church and study walls. But the end result is credibility and empathy that are only earned and discovered when we walk alongside our people.

5

The Preacher As Intercessor

Preaching week in and week out can be a grind. I remember hearing a veteran preacher refer to it this way, "You can only hit the same nail for so long before it gets old." I was younger when I heard his comment, and I remember thinking, *I can't imagine a day when I won't be absolutely energized by getting up to preach on a Sunday morning.* Now I know better.

Don't get me wrong. It's a worthy endeavor, and I feel undeniably called to it. But when you speak almost every week, sometimes multiple messages, it can start to wear you down. And when it does, my default is to focus more on content (What do I want to say?) than on my own spiritual engagement (Who do I want to be?).

So in the midst of the countdown to Sunday, I'm learning to bathe my sermons with these seven specific prayers. I wish I could tell you I pray these prayers diligently every week that I speak; I don't. But when I do, I'm better prepared to wrestle down what God is prompting me to say and deliver it with power and clarity.

Search Me

My 2004 Honda Civic isn't pretty, but it's paid off. I was vigilant about getting the oil changed every 3,000 miles, but now I need to fill the oil tank in between changes. The car is good about letting me know when it's ready for more; it starts lurching when I accelerate. The first time this happened, I was traveling across the state of Michigan and the car kept revving unexpectedly. I was able to nurse it back home, and the next day I took it into my local mechanic. He asked, "Does your car need oil to run?" He was being facetious. All cars do. Apparently, mine was struggling because it was almost completely empty. Once I realized I needed to fill the oil more often than I used to, the problem stopped. On occasion, I'll forget and the Civic starts heaving again. It's her gentle way of telling me she's running low. If I don't listen, she won't go.

Our call as preachers is to be fully devoted to Christ, fully alive to the text, and fully present in the pulpit. On our best days, we are. Then there are the rest of the days, when we lurch. Maybe we feel ourselves working from a sense of striving, not operating from a place of peace. Or we feel anxious, short-tempered, or spiritually fatigued. We often lack the self-awareness to diagnose what's going on at the soul level, what steps we need to take to get unstuck.

These are "search me" moments, turning points when we pause and ask God to tell us what he sees in us. The standard invitation for divine examination is Psalm 139. The writer starts the song with "You have searched me, Lord, and you know me" (v. 1). He admits God has already taken inventory of his heart, mind, and soul. At the end of the psalm though, he calls on God to do it again.

"Do I not hate those who hate you, Lord, and abhor those who are in rebellion against you? I have nothing but hatred for them; I count them my enemies. Search me, God, and know my heart; test me and know my anxious thoughts. See if there is any offensive way in me, and lead me in the way everlasting" (vv. 21–24).

I confess in the days before preaching, the prayers I'll pray are more "Please give me a fresh take on this passage" than "See if there is any offensive way in me." But if I have to choose between preaching a novel take on a text with an unexamined heart or a simple reading of the text with a clean heart, I will pick the latter. Every time.

I'm learning to pray, "Identify my points of resistance. Lead me in true confession."

As I write this, I've been working through the Gospel of Luke in my own regular Scripture reading. In Luke, we read a compelling, heart-searching story: the account of Jesus and an unnamed blind man. Jesus is approaching Jericho as the man sits near the road begging. As Jesus nears, he yells, "Jesus, Son of David, have mercy on me!" When others in the crowd tell him to quiet down, he escalates his demand and shouts again, "Son of David, have mercy on me!" Then Jesus stops and invites the man to come close before asking, "What do you want me to do for you?" (18:38–41).

At first glance, it almost seems like a cruel question. Is Jesus really going to make this man, who is already living on the margins, state an obvious request? In truth, Jesus is probing his heart. "Lord, have mercy," in this instance, anyway, is a generic prayer. Jesus is drilling for the raw, unfiltered truth, the deep yearning of this man's soul. Without hesitation, the man says, "I want to see." And Jesus grants his request.

I once heard someone say, "Specific prayers get specific answers." Sometimes, a "search me" prayer is answered not with a list of offenses and shortcomings, but with a penetrating question. Is it possible God is speaking to us through our desires? And that when we vocalize those desires, we find them either too small or truly bold? Could it be that God, as he searches us, peels back the socially acceptable veneer and pinpoints our hunger for notoriety, influence, and wealth?

Maybe the strongest component of the "search me" prayer is "I want to see." Lord, I want to see you as you are. I want to see me as

I am. Not as I want to project myself to you or others. I want to see our church as you do. I want to see our community, with its rich beauty and its deep brokenness. Show me what you see, because I dare not take up your Word without your perspective.

Teach Me

My natural inclination is to pursue topics, passages, or themes I already know. It's easier to preach a new angle on a familiar concept or recycle an older sermon altogether than to start from scratch. But whether I'm preaching an old idea or a new one, I need to pray, "Lord, teach me what you want me to teach." Maybe another way to phrase it is "Lord, preach to me in order to preach through me."

This is easily the scariest preaching prayer to pray, as it asks God to reveal the pressing issues in my own spiritual journey. I'd rather communicate without moving toward self-awareness, confession, and personal sacrifice, but to teach of God without learning anything from God is just another form of hypocrisy. "Lord, please don't let me preach a truth I'm not living, or at least not seeking to live."

In Jesus' final words to his disciples before his ascension, he compels them to go to the nations "and teach them to obey everything I have commanded you" (Matt. 28:20). Christ's assumption here is that the disciples are already obeying his commands. Before we call others to obey a scriptural mandate, it's fair to ask God to teach us to obey it and give us opportunities between now and Sunday to live this truth in our immediate context. The heart of the gospel transcends trick and tips. It propels us toward grounded and lasting transformation.

In academic research, there is a distinction between theoretical and applied knowledge in fields like physics, math, economics, and ethics. Theoretical research deals with abstract, hypothetical scenarios. Applied research addresses real-world problems. When it comes to prayer, a "search me" petition deals with themes; it asks, "God, what do you need me to know or to see?" A "teach me" request seeks help alchemizing knowledge into obedient action.

Moses prays this way: " 'If you are pleased with me, teach me your ways so I may know you and continue to find favor with you. Remember that this nation is your people.' The Lord replied, 'My Presence will go with you, and I will give you rest' " (Ex. 33:13–14). God doesn't give Moses a detailed list of instructions or burden him with the weight of problem solving. He promises his presence. The implication of that presence? Wisdom and rest.

In Psalm 119, the songwriter prays, "Teach me" no fewer than 12 times. Almost every 15 verses, we come back to the refrain, "Teach me, Lord, the way of your decrees, that I may follow it to the end" (v. 33). In the Hebrew model, knowledge isn't simply wisdom acquired; it is wisdom lived. In my own journey, as I've prepared for sermons, I've caught myself saying, "I've got this one." I have the language tools, the contextual background, insight from world-renowned professors, and examples from incredible historical preachers at my fingertips. But if I fail to pray "Teach me" and truly mean it, I'll end up parroting what others have said, with no lived experience of joyful obedience.

Lead Me

After I ask God to take inventory of my heart and educate my mind, I invite God to lead my preaching process. It's another petition I borrow from the psalmists. They petition for wisdom on each step of their journey:

> "Lead me, Lord, in your righteousness because of my enemies—make your way straight before me." (Ps. 5:8)

> "Since you are my rock and my fortress, for the sake of your name lead and guide me." (Ps. 31:3)

> "Send me your light and your faithful care, let them lead me; let them bring me to your holy mountain, to the place where you dwell." (Ps. 43:3)

Note their motives here. They need divine leadership so they can honor God's name and experience God's presence. I'm learning to pray, "Lead me in each moment of study. I need to sense your presence at every point in my preparation time."

The good news about having a study routine is it keeps us focused and anchored in a sustainable rhythm. But one potential pitfall of working off such a schedule is it can become rote and dull. I can work through my sermon preparation checklist and still fail to capture the specific message God may have for our community.

Yes, quantity of time matters, but invariably there will be weeks when we end up with less time than we budgeted. There are hospital visits and funerals and board meetings that go long. Or I just procrastinate. As much as I want to believe I had a great preparation and study plan, sometimes I'm not feeling it and it's hard to get the words on the page.

In these moments, I've often leaned on the words of Proverbs 16:3: "Commit to the Lord whatever you do, and he will establish your plans." That leads me to pray, "Lord, I don't love what I have here. It's not what I worked for, hoped for, or imagined in my mind's eye. But it's what I have now, and I'm committing it to you. Establish it as only you can and use it for your purposes."

Anoint Me

Both Isaiah, while preaching in Judea, and Jesus, while speaking in Galilee, declared, "The Spirit of the Sovereign Lord is on me, because the Lord has anointed me to proclaim good news to the poor. He has sent me to bind up the brokenhearted, to proclaim freedom for the captives and release from darkness for the prisoners" (Isa. 61:1; Luke 4:18). Apparently, both preachers believed the Spirit plays a critical role in specific preaching moments. Peter echoes this sentiment when he writes, "... prophets, though human, spoke from God as they were carried along by the Holy Spirit" (2 Pet. 1:21).

The prayer here is, "Spirit of God, I can craft this message, but I need you to carry it. When I finally step into the pulpit, anoint the delivery of this message."

When I'm not careful and I feel comfortable with my material, I can be guilty of ordinary public speaking with biblical content. Instead, I want to be ever mindful of what the Spirit is doing in and around me throughout the very act of preaching.

Have you ever been at a worship service where the pastor, after ascending the steps to the podium, says, "I had a message prepared for today, but I feel the Lord has given me something else to say"? I confess the cynic in me questions if there was ever an original sermon to begin with, or if this is sloppy preaching cloaked in the guise of "being sensitive to the Spirit." However, if there's no supernatural dimension to our preaching, if every time, we arrive believing we've managed the uncontrollable fire of God like a tiger on a tight leash, then something's wrong.

God doesn't owe the preacher anything. But I believe God works in spite of me, not because of me, more often than I choose to admit. So, this prayer goes something like this: "When I stand up to preach, do what I can't. Bridge the gap. Fill what is lacking. Infuse this message with power, and at the moment of delivery, if I've prepared something that ought not to be said, give me grace to let it go. And if there's a word of rebuke, challenge, or encouragement that becomes clear to me in the preaching moment, give me courage to declare it."

Prepare Them

Jesus' parable of the sower is a great gift to preachers. He reminds us that while we can cast seed, only he can shape the soil. Jesus reveals three obstacles hearers face: spiritual confusion, spiritual tribulation, and spiritual insecurity.

Some listeners who will hear your words this weekend are living in a spiritual upside-down world. They lack fundamental clarity to appreciate who God is and what the kingdom looks like. And the Evil One snatches wisdom away. Others are still very fresh on their spiritual journey. They're excited about where they are and believe the words of God and the moving of the Spirit to be real, but the presence of trouble and persecution (which Jesus says are fully guaranteed on our earthly pilgrimage) are squeezing the joy out of their lives. The third group may not be drowning in tribulation, but they fear what they can't control. The pursuit of personal control and the belief that just a little more cash will calm them keep choking out the words of life they hear.

Watchman Nee once said that intercession is someone prayed to, someone prayed for, and someone prayed against. The "prepare them" prayer is offered to the Father; for those who come to hear the Word but struggle with confusion, fatigue, or anxiety; and against the Evil One, whom Jesus names in this parable.

About 30 minutes before a service begins, I try to imagine where the people who may be in attendance are and what they're thinking. So, at 8:30 a.m. or 10:00 a.m. on a Sunday morning, I picture young parents buckling their kids into a minivan or a couple of empty nesters finishing breakfast at their favorite diner. There's a teenager whose parents are threatening or bribing them to get out of bed and ready for church. There's a father who lost his job on Friday. There's a grandmother who just heard her chemotherapy treatments weren't effective. All of them come with different thoughts, needs, and expectations.

So I pray, "Lord, prepare their hearts. Not to receive my thoughts, but to hear your voice. Meet them at their point of greatest need. Till the soil of their soul, so that, if they choose to, they might welcome the seed you would sow."

Change Us

It used to be "Lord, change them." But I'm not an unmoved actor in the preaching process. I'm not an unconscious delivery agent of some transcendent spiritual truth. The preacher is not static in the act of preaching; he or she is a fluid, organic participant in both the speaking and the hearing of the Word.

God doesn't transform the preacher so that, through him or her, the gathered hearers might be transformed. I believe that God, rather than leading the preacher and the people on parallel tracks at varying paces, looks to take a unified, local church body on a singular journey. So, the prayer can't be a cop-out—"Lord, change these people, for they are broken." Instead I can pray, "Lord, change us together, that we might be a collective prophetic voice in the context of our homes, schools, businesses, and city."

I don't think God's intent for preaching is for dialogue about the text to be reduced to "Nice sermon, Pastor" in the narthex or "So, what did you think about the sermon?" over lunch. If the sum of a congregation's engagement with a sermon is "Did I like it?" or "Did I find it intellectually stimulating?" we're undervaluing the power of Scripture and the importance of communal reflection.

One possible "change us" prayer a community can pray after

preaching is: "Lord, what does my life look like if what we've heard is true? What actions should result from our collective obedience? Is it individual and/or corporate repentance? Is it a careful communal discernment process? What does it look like for us to embody this truth together over the next weeks, months, or years?"

The tricky part of the "change us" prayer is that it may, in fact, require us to change. Have you heard the one about the congregant who complains to the preacher, "I feel like we heard this sermon last week"? The preacher responds, "And you'll hear it again next week and the week after until we start living it." It could be that a particular message, text, call, or theme will land so powerfully in a congregation that a return to business as usual would be cavalier.

If the goal of preaching is proclamation that results in transformation, it's the preacher's job to identify markers of communal change. And if a particular sermon creates spiritual traction in a church, it may require changing tack. It could mean exploring a theme in depth and shelving next week's preaching plan for a future date.

I used to wonder, "What happens if we preach and people don't change?" Now I ask, "What happens if we preach and they do? Are we ready to pivot? To lead? To redirect?"

Protect Me

1 Kings 18–19 paints dramatically different portraits of Elijah. In chapter 18, he boldly calls the nation of Israel together, confidently challenges the prophet of Baal, and dramatically calls fire down from heaven. And to finish a compelling day of ministry, he outruns Ahab's horses on the way to Jezreel—in the rain. It's the stuff of legend.

Chapter 19 begins with Jezebel's promise to kill Elijah. So Elijah runs for his life, and when he gets to the Judean desert, he tells

God, "I have had enough, Lord. Take my life; I am no better than my ancestors" (v. 4). Elijah goes from a literal and figurative mountaintop to the pit of despair.

Granted, most of us have not had our lives threatened as a result of our preaching. Nevertheless, the Elijah account is worth considering. For me, preaching is both animating and consuming. Preaching is marked by a sense of deep awe, a total emotional investment, and a surge of spiritual adrenaline. I struggle to sit down for very long before I preach, and it can take me a few hours to decompress after the preaching is done.

I learned that when I am physically, emotionally, and spiritually depleted, I can land in a vulnerable spot. If I feel fatigue, I can drift toward numbness or melancholy. If I feel like things went well, I might lean toward an inflated ego.

As a new preacher, my primary focus was on avoiding doctrinal error. And this concern is right and good. James says, "Not many of you should become teachers, my fellow believers, because you know that we who teach will be judged more strictly. We all stumble in many ways. Anyone who is never at fault in what they say is perfect, able to keep their whole body in check" (James 3:1–2). As a result, I prayed for protection before I spoke, protection from error.

Decades later, I'm also praying for protection after I speak, protection from myself and from evil. The worst version of me, the one that ties "successful" preaching to self-worth, needs to hear from Proverbs and Peter:

> "When pride comes, then comes disgrace, but with humility comes wisdom." (Prov. 11:2)
>
> "In the same way, you who are younger, submit yourselves to your elders. All of you, clothe yourselves with

> humility toward one another, because, 'God opposes the proud but shows favor to the humble.' Humble yourselves, therefore, under God's mighty hand, that he may lift you up in due time." (1 Pet. 5:5-6)

When the preaching is done, it's not uncommon to be tempted toward believing our own hype, thinking that if something powerful transpired, it was achieved by our wit, our work, our wooing. In these moments, we must recognize humility is a muscle that grows with use, that a humble heart is the product of reflection, surrender, perspective, and input from trusted friends.

And evil? Jesus says to pray, "Lead us not into temptation, but deliver us from the evil one" (Matt. 6:13). A mentor once told me, "Pride isn't just thinking too highly of yourself. It can also be thinking too little of yourself. Either way, the focus is on you."

I've had some strange moments where, either hours or days after preaching, I've felt alone, afraid, and uncertain. In these moments I, like Elijah, can be spiritually fragile and prone to detaching emotionally and spiritually in the name of "rest and recovery." But Sabbath rest is fruitful and filling; mindlessly watching TV is not. So, I've had to be intentional about praying for protection and strategic about the kind of post-preaching routines that keep me plugged into Christ and authentic in community with others.

It could be only a few of these prayers resonate with you. That's okay as long as you find your own set of prayers, based on your style, personality, and struggles. You can't stop Sunday from coming, but you can be primed and ready when it gets here.

6

The Preacher As Artist

When I was 30, I suffered what doctors call a spontaneous pneumothorax. My lung suddenly collapsed and it was difficult to breathe. I had to spend a few days at the hospital, and friends would drop in to help me pass the time. One friend, Chris, brought a book of Mad Libs. Mad Libs are stories with certain words left out. One person asks another to offer certain kinds of words—nouns, verbs, adverbs, and adjectives—and then puts them in their respective places in the story. Hilarity ensues when both parties read the completed, nonsensical story.

For too many years, I saw preaching like a Mad Libs-esque exercise. There was a standard format, and all I needed to do was fill in the blanks. Every tradition and style has its own blanks, but we all have a template we work from. Here are some of the blanks I was working with at the time:

Start with a Joke

Of course, humor is disarming and breaks down barriers. There's definitely a place for joy in the preaching moment, especially since we live in anxious times. There's a difference, however, between a shared human moment and a quest for self-serving laughs. In my context, the joke was intended to make the preacher likable early in the sermon. In hindsight, I realize this might make for a great corporate presentation but can undermine great preaching.

Use Scripture, But Not too Much

Do you remember the quote from the itinerant speaker in Chapter 1? The itinerant speaker said, "I've got a great sermon. Now I just need some verses to go with it." This school of thought says audiences can't be trusted with more than a few disconnected verses in a 30-minute timespan and it's best to spoon-feed easy-to-swallow gospel maxims, even if it means ignoring the context. Paul tells Timothy to devote himself to the "public reading of Scripture" (1 Tim. 4:13). Sometimes the act of preaching includes declaring the text in chunks, not in sound bites.

Tell a Self-Revelatory Anecdote

Include a story about a struggle that makes you accessible. The more dramatic, the better. It doesn't have to be current. Just have one or two in your pocket so people can know "You're human too." Of course, if we fully embraced the doctrine of the priesthood of all believers, the congregation would already believe the preacher was human before he or she even stepped into the pulpit. These stories would be redundant.

Make Scripture Come Alive

I affirm the sentiment behind this thought. I know what people are hoping to say, but the premise is faulty. It starts with the idea that the text is stagnant and it's the preacher's job to resuscitate it.

Always Be Closing

Again, this instruction is well-intended. However, sometimes the response the preacher is asking for isn't connected to the passage at hand. There's some other agenda, either conscious or unconscious, in play. I preached in one environment where the finance team required that the offering be taken after the sermon because "people give more when they are moved emotionally." Of course, no one came right out and said it, but it was difficult to shake the thought that the preaching was primarily viewed as revenue generator.

I'm sure you have "blanks" you could add to this list from your own experience, tradition, and context.

'Homiletical Pragmatism'

In *The Preacher as Liturgical Artist,* Trygve Johnson coins the phrase "homiletical pragmatism." It's the idea that if the preacher follows a certain formula, he or she can move people to a specific result. Johnson calls this

> . . . the utilitarian use of words and rhetoric based on the assumption that preaching is a matter of finding the right presentational technique. The proper technique is seen to be done without surrendering one's words and oneself to the presence and work of the Word and the Spirit.[1]

The Mad Libs model is the hallmark of homiletical pragmatism. Humans select words. Organize those words. Craft, shape, and mold the words and then declare them to the congregation. If we're not careful, we'll strip preaching from its divine element, its supernatural dimension, in the name of efficacy.

I preached versions of Mad Libs sermons for years. Then the angst set in. I remember feeling that as much as I wanted to be true

[1] Trygve David Johnson, *The Preacher as Liturgical Artist: Metaphor, Identity, and the Vicarious Humanity of Christ* (Eugene: Cascade Books, 2014), 86.

to the text, the shadow mission in my preaching was for people to like me, like the church, and prove it with their continued attendance and giving. There were Sundays where I followed the script I had, people smiled appreciatively and went home, seemingly the same people they were when they walked in. We all went home and repeated the cycle. Again and again and again.

In hindsight, my view of preaching was flawed. I saw myself as a content delivery vehicle and the people as spiritual content consumers. That's it. Preaching was merely the transfer of spiritual information from one point to the next. We weren't partners in a dance, where the truth and character of God were the music; we were just numbers in an equation with a fixed outcome.

Many well-meaning communications books and homiletics professors give us templates to craft coherent sermons. If we view preaching like a chemistry experiment, as a closed system with a clear formula and predictable results, our preaching will be formulaic and predictable.

I remember taking chemistry as a sophomore in high school. I was a dutiful student, but the lab experiments were tedious. Sure, they let us use a Bunsen burner, but we never got to watch it do anything fun or exciting. One day, however, in a lecture on an element in the periodic table, our young teacher showed us a video of what happens when you put cesium in water: it explodes. Almost every day after that my friend Joel and I would ask Mrs. Thompson if she could get us some cesium. She always refused.

I didn't want to do the stock chemistry experiments, I wanted to throw a stick of cesium into a sink and watch the reaction. Too often, I've been guilty of treating my preaching like a lab "experiment" where there's no real discovery. We follow the script, hoping we'll get the right answer and a good grade.

Instead, I want to view preaching like that 16-year-old desperate for cesium. I know how it's supposed to work; I want to see it in action for myself. I want to come to the preaching moment believing there's something explosive, something truly transformative in the text, and speak into a room with two parts hydrogen and one part oxygen and see what happens.

Is There a Recipe for Preaching?

I think we need to reframe the preacher as a creative force, an artist. Not as a line cook at a fast-food restaurant, following the pictures on a card, but as a master chef playing with different ingredients in the quest of something transcendent.

In the Disney-Pixar film *Ratatouille,* Linguine is a garbage boy at a famous Parisian restaurant. Through an odd series of circumstances, he is given the opportunity to create dishes in the kitchen. Colette, the *chef de partie,* is assigned to show him how to cook the kitchen's best dishes. Their conversation goes like this:

> Colette: I know the Gusteau style code. In every dish, Chef Gusteau always had something unexpected. I will show you. I memorized all his recipes.
> Linguini: (taking notes) Always do something unexpected…
> Colette: No! Follow the recipe!
> Linguini: But you said to—
> Colette: No. It was *his* job to be unexpected. It is *our* job to follow the recipe.[2]

Artistry requires risk, innovation, and experimentation. Sometimes that sounds exhilarating, and sometimes it sounds exhausting. Our default as preachers, especially those of us schooled in homiletical

[2] Brad Bird, dir., *Ratatouille* (Los Angeles: Walt Disney Pictures/Pixar Animation Studio, 2007), DVD.

pragmatism, is to simply follow the recipe.

Here's the problem. Although there are many proven and effective principles for communication, there is no firm recipe for preaching. At least, Jesus doesn't offer us one.

In his *Reflections on the Psalms*, C. S. Lewis points out,

> We may observe that the teaching of Our Lord Himself, in which there is no imperfection, is not given us in that cut-and-dried, fool-proof, systematic fashion we might have expected or desired. He wrote no book. We have only reported sayings, most of them uttered in answer to questions, shaped in some degree by their context. And when we have collected them all we cannot reduce them to a system. He preaches but He does not lecture.[3]

"He preaches but He does not lecture." And aren't we glad he did?

Jesus spoke in different ways to different people at different times for different reasons. His preaching to the religious elite had a distinct tone, dissimilar from the one he used to engage with sinners and tax collectors. Some parables were only explained in private to the disciples. Some messages were met with hostility (the men at the synagogue in Nazareth tried to kill Jesus after his first message).

After gathering huge crowds, Jesus' message in Capernaum thins out the crowds. John 6:60 and 66 tell us, "On hearing it, many of his disciples said, 'This is a hard teaching. Who can accept it?' . . . From this time many of his disciples turned back and no longer followed him." Some sermons were only a sentence or two long. "The kingdom of God has come near. Repent and believe the good news!" (Mark 1:15). Others required people to sit out in the open for hours and potentially miss a daily meal.

[3] C. S. Lewis, *Reflections on the Psalms* (New York: Harper One, 2017), 131.

Jesus seems to employ tactics and methods that don't make sense and certainly don't generate predictable responses. Yet, Jesus' preaching was incredibly effective. It did everything he intended it to do over the course of his public ministry.

Blueprint or Canvas

Maybe that's the beauty of seeing the preacher as an artist. We're not painting single portraits in isolation, one sermon at a time. We're painting a mural over the course of a lifetime, communicating big-picture themes about who God is, who God declares us to be, and what it means to walk in light of these truths.

My friend Alex McManus once said when it comes to preaching, there are builders and there are painters. Builders begin with a blueprint. Then they follow it with focus. They build a foundation, put up a frame, install the plumbing, wire the electricity, put up drywall, and add exterior siding with mathematical precision. Painters, however, start with a blank canvas. They want to convey something visceral, something beautiful, an image that provokes questions, inspires wonder, or portrays hope to all who ultimately behold the image. For me, I want to see preaching more like an oil painting rather than structural engineering.

If all we need to preach is the ability to grasp the finer points of Greek rhetoric, we could be content with the Pauline Epistles. We can parse Paul's style and mimic his tone. To be sure, Paul's preaching is a compelling and viable model. But he's one preacher among many in the Bible. The deceptively simple parables, the layered emotions of the psalms, the visceral pleading of the prophets, and the nuanced narratives in the Gospels and historical books, invite us to explore a broad palette of colors and rich array of media.

If the preacher is to be more than scribe, copying words and phrases from an ancient scroll, what does a preacher as artist look like? What practices ought the preacher pursue to cultivate his or her creative dimension?

The Journey of a Preacher As Artist

My friend Nate Young is the senior vice president of design and innovation for a leading global consumer goods company. He also served as the executive vice president and chief academic officer at Art Center College of Design in Pasadena, California. I asked Nate what preachers can learn from artists. He recommended American art educator Betty Edwards's creative process as outlined in her 1979 book *Drawing on the Right Side of the Brain.*[4] The six-step journey includes: observation, investigation, incubation, solution, decision, and validation.

Observation

The first visceral step in the process is observation. In this phase, the artist explores and examines creation, events, objects, scenes, and people. In preaching, sometimes the Spirit invites us to take a closer look at an ordinary event and look beyond it. In Jeremiah's case, God sent him to the potter's house to observe an unspectacular act and look for rich spiritual insight.

In preaching, sometimes the observation includes insights or questions from examining the text (independent of sermon preparation), watching a relationship, grieving a loss, celebrating a milestone, or engaging in spiritual practices. Like the artist, the preacher is actively watching people, circumstances, and his or her own emotions, to discern "What does God want me to see or know in this instance?"

Observation is a skill that grows with practice. Just as many

[4] Betty Edwards, *Drawing on the Right Side of the Brain: A Course in Enhancing Creativity and Artistic Confidence* (New York: Tarcher Perigree, 2012), 249–253.

artists keep a sketchbook on hand for ideas and images, preachers who think like artists have notebooks or files they use to collect observations they want to revisit. At a workshop for preachers and teachers, someone asked Ken Davis, "How do you know which image or experience to write down?" He responded, "Capture anything that moves you."

If it sparks curiosity, wonder, joy, scorn, sadness, anything that touches the range of human emotion, write it down and add it to the list. Ken said that as he was driving from the airport to the conference center, something on the road caught his attention. A road crew had been painting lines on the highway and had painted a line directly over the body of a dead rodent. Ken laughed. "I don't know what I'm going to use that story for, but I'm writing it down!"

When it comes to observing a text, we submit ourselves to it. Bruce Herman, professor of art and gallery director at Gordon College, says, "If you want to 'understand' something, you have to be willing to 'stand under' it."[5] Scripture is less like a pencil that an artist holds and more like a horizon that the artist beholds. It's helpful to consider C. S. Lewis' instruction from *An Experiment in Criticism*: "We sit down before the picture in order to have something done to us, not that we may do things with it. The first demand of any work of art makes upon us is surrender. Look. Listen. Receive. Get yourself out of the way."[6]

Investigation

Investigation is the attempt to find out why something is the way it is. Nate Young cautions against skipping observation to get to investigation. Our instinct to find the answer to a question can

[5] Makoto Fujimura, *Refractions: A Journey of Faith, Art, and Culture* (Colorado Springs: NavPress, 2009), 148.

[6] C. S. Lewis, *An Experiment in Criticism* (Cambridge: Cambridge University Press, 1992), *18-19.*

shortcut the valuable time required to watch, to wait, to listen. In art and preaching, research serves to fill the gaps in our knowledge of the subject matter.

The computer animators who created Disney-Pixar's 2003 film *Finding Nemo* pursued a multidisciplinary approach to their investigation phase. They took a course in marine biology, studied underwater camera footage from marine experts, and spent time scuba diving in the Pacific.[7]

For many preachers, the formal education process was research intensive. The digital revolution offers preachers more tools (commentaries, dictionaries, lexicons) for research than have ever been available at any point in human history. In fact, the temptation for some of us is to get lost in the sea of research as we chase down data from multiple sources. The challenge then is knowing when to stop investigating.

Incubation

Incubation is what Nate calls "the hardest and most skipped step." It's the part of the process where artists put their right brain to work. Nate says once he poses a creative question and identifies a deadline to produce something, he gives his brain space to ask, "Have you found anything yet?" Nate drives an hour each way to his office every workday. This isn't an inconvenience; it's part of his creative process. Creatives understand the value of taking a drive, mowing the lawn, staying open to insights that spark in the shower.

Incubation cultivates opportunities for breakthrough or *Aha!* moments. But Nate warns against jumping at the first compelling insight. If we get impatient in the incubation phase, we end up

[7] Gary Dretzka, " 'Nemo' animators got all wet / Intense analysis helped team re-create water on computer," *San Francisco Gate*, Jan. 2012. Accessed on October 28, 2020. https://www.sfgate.com/bayarea/article/Nemo-animators-got-all-wet-Intense-analysis-2614973.php.

landing on solutions that are familiar. Over time, our work starts to feel redundant and derivative. If you don't like what you have, let your idea incubate some more.

In his book *Steal Like an Artist: 10 Things Nobody Told You About Being Creative,* Austin Kleon says,

> Creative people need time to just sit around and do nothing. I get some of my best ideas when I'm bored, which is why I never take my shirts to the cleaners. I love ironing my shirts—it's so boring, I almost always get good ideas. If you're out of ideas, wash the dishes. Take a really long walk. Stare at a spot on the wall for as long as you can. As the artist Maira Kalman says, "Avoiding work is the way to focus my mind."[8]

The idea of incubation is personally liberating. Years ago, I interviewed for a preaching job at a church. The senior pastor asked me, "How much time do you spend preparing your sermons?" For me, it's always felt like a trick question because it's hard to quantify incubation. If I answer "It takes me two hours" to write a sermon, it can sound like I'm (a) lazy (this interviewer couldn't fathom anything less than 15 hours), or (b) brilliant (only a savant can produce a coherent message in so brief a period). But this is a false dichotomy. It presupposes that only time in the study counts for sermon prep. In truth, if we believe in incubation, every time our right brain is engaged, even if it's on a day off, we're "working" on a sermon.

---

[8] Austin Kleon, *Steal Like an Artist: 10 Things Nobody Told You About Being Creative* (New York: Workman Publishing Company, 2012), 67.

Solution

Solution is the turning point in the process. Often, a deadline or other creative constraint is what helps drive the timing and shape of a solution. A solution can surface when we understand what resources are available to us in a given scenario. If your tradition uses the lectionary, you have a built-in boundary around your sermon thinking. Sometimes, based on other events on the church calendar, your theme shifts or the time available for the preaching moment changes.

Austin Kleon observes, "The right constraints can lead to your very best work. My favorite example? Dr. Seuss wrote *The Cat in the Hat* with only 236 different words, so his editor bet him he couldn't write a book with only 50 words. Dr. Seuss came back and won the bet with *Green Eggs and Ham*, one of the bestselling children's books of all time."[9]

And Jack White, the American singer, songwriter, and producer, says, "Telling yourself you have all the time in the world, all the money in the world, all the colors in the palette, anything you want—that just kills creativity."[10] The solution comes at the intersection of our talents and experiences, available resources and materials, and in the case of preaching, the chosen text.

Decision

Decision is the execution phase. According to Nate, this the shortest step in the creative process. It's the moment "you're going to be resolute with your answer." This is the moment when the artist actively begins drawing, sculpting, filming, or writing. As a preacher, this is when I lock myself in the study with my laptop and don't come out until the sermon is done.

---

[9] Kleon, 138.
[10] Ibid.

Part of the discipline of art, and preaching, is to determine when exactly we'll implement our solution. In Steven Pressfield's work, *The War of Art,* he recounts, "Someone once asked Somerset Maugham if he wrote on a schedule or only when struck by inspiration. 'I write only when inspiration strikes,' he replied. 'Fortunately it strikes every morning at nine o'clock sharp.' "[11]

If the "when" of decision matters, the "where" it takes place does too. Makoto Fujimura in his work *Refractions* says,

> I am often asked, "How do you juggle family, ministry, and your art all at the same time?" Many people have a hard time keeping their creative side alive in the busyness of our times. The advice I give is to dedicate a space, even a small desk, for working on nothing other than your art, whatever medium that may be. Guard against other parts of your life invading that dedicated space. Then, I advise them, to do what Dana Gioia did: Make yourself sit down in front of that dedicated space. If you're a poet, like him, copy the last stanza of what you wrote; if you're a visual artist, open the sketchbook and look at what you have done.[12]

For the preacher, the decision step is twofold. There is the decision to write the sermon and then the decision to deliver the sermon: Sermon writing and sermon giving are complementary but distinct acts. Based on personal wiring, family of origin, and faith tradition, we will likely favor one aspect over the other. Both, however, require investment, energy, and the will to execute them well.

---

[11] Steven Pressfield *The War of Art: Break Through the Blocks and Win Your Inner Creative Battles,* (New York: Black Irish Entertainment, 2002), 64.
[12] Fujimura, 16.

Validation

Validation asks, "Does the completed work solve the observation? Did it validate everything you did?" Validation is the reflection on the process and the result. Young reminds me that this step isn't helpful in every process.

In fact, while it's useful for some artists in some disciplines, it's potentially harmful for the preacher. The sermon isn't validated by the hearer or even the preacher. The Word stands on its own and invariably will unsettle or disturb the preachers or the listeners. To revisit the parable of the sower, the only validating question to pose is: Did the preacher sow the seed he or she was given to sow? Did you steward your call and gifts to bear witness to the character of God or not?

I don't want to pursue preaching in which God has a bit part. I don't want to spend years honing technique at the expense of creating room for God's power to break through.

We can practice throwing a ball into the water with perfect form. Our mechanics can be flawless, but if there's no power in it beyond our own communication skills and wordsmithing, there will be a splash but no fireworks. Only cesium explodes on contact with water. Only Spirit-infused preaching yields moments that initiate transformation.

So rather than picking up a pencil to fill in a predictable blank, let's pick up a paintbrush to create an image so compelling that it sparks people to wonder and worship, to dancing and dreaming.

7

The Preacher As Coach

Pastors protect their pulpits. That's not wrong. Paul admonishes Timothy and Titus to guard against false teachers and questionable doctrine. But sometimes pastors defend their pulpit not from heresy but from any voice that isn't theirs.

In my high school years, I attended a fast-growing suburban megachurch, a beacon for growth, evangelism, and missions in our denomination. It was rare for the senior pastor to be away on a Sunday morning, but when he was, it was almost certain one of his friends would travel from out of town to preach. Occasionally, one of the associate pastors would preach on a Wednesday or Sunday evening service. But primetime preaching was reserved for the senior pastor or honored guests.

Early in my vocational ministry, the church I worked for had a team-teaching approach. Three primary preachers would rotate through Sunday morning and Wednesday night teaching. Every once in a while, associate pastors would pinch-hit on a "low-risk" Sunday morning. (If you've ever been the youth pastor who preached Sunday morning on a Fourth of July, Thanksgiving, or the Sunday after Christmas, you're not alone.) As the church grew to a multisite model, they retained their commitment to team teaching. When they added a second and third campus, they used the preachers on staff. But when it was time for campuses four through eight, they hired outside preachers.

Both scenarios share a common thread: the need for gifted and trusted preachers to help carry the load. In the first scenario, my perception is that the senior pastor didn't trust his associates to fill his shoes in his absence. In the second scenario, the only one I can speak to authoritatively, it was easier for the church to hire outside talent than it was to raise new preachers up to meet the preaching demand.

Many preachers spend more time in their study than they do identifying, encouraging, and equipping other preachers. As a result, they struggle with unnecessary fatigue and fail to elevate unique voices within their context. I've used plenty of excuses over the years for not investing in emerging preachers, from the obvious ones—"I don't have time" and "It's easier for me to do it myself"—to the frightening ones—"I'm afraid I might get upstaged," "Nobody can do it as well as I can," "No one else knows these people like I do," "I've talked for so long; I don't know how to listen to someone else."

In the end, they're all still excuses. Even if you're not a natural people developer, there's a moral imperative and a biblical mandate for you to invest in emerging preachers. So let's explore both why the preacher should function as a coach and how the preacher can function as a coach.

Shared Calling to a Shared Service

Many of us were developed in systems that empowered and celebrated preachers as called individuals who serve as individuals. Yet, the scriptures present multiple examples of people who are called and mobilized in pairs or teams.

When God calls Moses in the far side of the wilderness, Moses balks at the mission. Even though God promises Moses his message will be received, Moses contends he's ill equipped for the task. He argues that he's "slow of speech and tongue" (Ex. 4:10). God's suggestion? "Don't carry the message alone. Get your big brother Aaron to speak with you" (paraphrase of Ex. 4:14–16).

For years I thought Aaron was Moses' spokesperson, and Moses, by divine prompting, was the speechwriter. But I missed a detail in Exodus 4:15. God says, "You [Moses] shall speak to him [Aaron] and put words in his mouth; I will help both of you speak and will teach you what to do." The phrase I overlooked was "I will help both of you speak." We can argue that from the very moment God institutionalized regular "preaching" to a congregation, the design was for the message to be declared to a community (Israel) in community (Moses, Aaron, and Miriam—called a prophet in Exodus 15:20).

This scene, a shared calling to a shared service, repeats in Matthew 4:18–19: "As Jesus was walking beside the Sea of Galilee, he saw two brothers, Simon called Peter and his brother Andrew. They were casting a net into the lake, for they were fishermen. 'Come, follow me,' Jesus said, 'and I will send you out to fish for people.'" And then again in Matthew 4:21, "Going on from there, he saw two other brothers, James son of Zebedee and his brother John."

In each of these instances, people are called in teams to grow in understanding God's heart and wisdom and then are sent out in teams, to declare what they know. Luke 10:1–2 says, "After this the Lord appointed seventy-two others and sent them two by two ahead of him to every town and place where he was about to go. He told them, 'The harvest is plentiful, but the workers are few. Ask the Lord of the harvest, therefore, to send out workers into his harvest field.'"

For all the examples of paired preaching and service in Scripture, educational and organizational institutions usually ordain people in groups and then send them out alone. In these instances, formal preaching training is limited to a specific time frame and delegated to approved trainers. This can be a good and valid starting point. I'm forever grateful for the preaching training I benefited from in my undergraduate and seminary experiences. That said, not every called preacher has access to these opportunities, and even those who do can benefit from ongoing coaching and encouragement.

The Old Testament offers two models for coaching preachers: individualized mentoring at an early age and communal training for adults. The first example is the Eli-Samuel relationship, and the second is the Elijah-Elisha model.

Individualized Mentoring

First Samuel recounts the story of Hannah and Elkanah's prayer for a son. When God answers their prayer in the child Samuel, his parents dedicate him to priestly service. Initially, Samuel comes to Shiloh to assist in priestly duties. Samuel's an Ephraimite, not a Levite.

The ministry succession plan for Eli is already established. When he retires or dies, his sons will step into his role. Except—"Eli's sons were scoundrels; they had no regard for the Lord" (1 Sam. 2:12). They steal meat from those offering sacrifices and sleep with the female servants at the tent of meeting. Eli may have been a good pastor, but he was failing as a father. And so badly that a man of God comes to Eli and prophesies that no one in his house will reach old age and the mantle of ministry will get handed to someone else.

All this happens while the child Samuel is serving Eli in his work. Though Samuel is familiar with the mechanics of ministry, he doesn't know the One he serves. The story tells us, "Now Samuel did not yet know the Lord: The word of the Lord had not yet been revealed to him.... Then Eli realized that the Lord was calling the boy. So Eli told Samuel, 'Go and lie down, and if he calls you, say, "Speak, Lord, for your servant is listening" ' " (1 Sam. 3:7, 8–9). If Eli's first gift to Samuel was introducing him to public ministry, his greatest gift was coaching him in how to discern God's voice.

Samuel already knows the value of the text. He's surely seen Eli examine and follow the Torah in his priestly service. And Samuel may be aware that God speaks to others. If Samuel was Eli's attendant, it's possible Samuel was present when the man of God delivered his messages to Eli. While Samuel can relay the message of the text or parrot God's words to others, he's never heard God speak to him.

Eli's coaching to young Samuel says,

- It seems like God is speaking directly to you.
- Here's how to adopt a receptive and engaged posture of listening.

Samuel follows Eli's instructions and does indeed hear from God. It's a brief and brutal message. The closing line of the message: No sacrifice can atone for the guilt of Eli's house (1 Sam. 3:14). I don't remember the exact text or tone of my first sermon, but I know it wasn't this. Not only is the content of Samuel's message harsh, he has the added challenge of having to deliver it to his boss, guardian, mentor, and father figure.

Maybe that's why the text doesn't say, "Samuel went back to sleep." It just says, "Samuel lay down until morning (v. 15)," likely staring at the ceiling in silence, struggling to figure out his next move. And in the morning, Eli, in his wisdom, asks Samuel to repeat what he heard. Because Eli could read the fear on Samuel face, he says, "Do not hide it from me. May God deal with you, be it ever so severely, if you hide from me anything he told you" (v. 17).

As a mentor, Eli knew it's not enough to know the truth of God. The preacher must declare it, even when—especially when—it's a hard truth to receive. Samuel's first step of faith was to say "Speak, Lord"; his next act of courage was to say, *Listen, Eli. These are the words of the Lord.* In its purest form, this is preaching: to hear and to speak. To listen in faith and refuse to hide in fear.

Through Eli's coaching, Samuel learns that this listening and speaking can become a learned habit. I've heard a saying that goes something like this, "Listening and obeying the voice of God is like a muscle. The more you practice it, the stronger it gets. When you fail to discern and proclaim the Word of God, the muscle atrophies." It's no accident that God spoke to Eli through an unnamed man of God and through a child. Eli wasn't hearing God anymore. His failure to obey what he knew to do dulled his ears to God's voice. Though God wasn't speaking to him, he knew enough to help Samuel discern God's voice.

The result was the emergence of one of Israel's storied prophets. The writer of 1 Samuel says, "The Lord was with Samuel as he grew up, and he let none of Samuel's words fall to the ground. . . . The Lord continued to appear at Shiloh, and there he revealed himself to Samuel through his word" (1 Sam. 3:19, 21).[1] Every Samuel has an Eli. Even if the mentor is flawed, he or she can still show emerging preachers the basics of listening to and proclaiming God's voice.

Growing up, my family attended church regularly. We were there on Wednesday nights and Sunday mornings. When I was in high school, my youth pastor, Darrin Hughes, helped me identify my capacity and desire to preach. It was he who first encouraged me to pursue a preaching development program within our denomination. At 16, I started putting together short sermons and devotional thoughts. Over the next two years, I realized I enjoyed the process

[1] While Samuel was a faithful leader, like Eli, he failed as a father (see 1 Sam. 8:1–5).

and the act of preaching.

In my college years, my youth ministry professor, Phil Collins, gave me assignments to prepare sermons for high school students and opportunities to preach messages for his youth group. After my second year at college, I did a summer internship with my former middle school pastor, Doug Brodess, who was then a senior pastor in Tucson. Under Doug's direction, I gave my first full Sunday morning sermon from John 13. In my final year of college, Chuck Gifford was my de facto preaching coach. Chuck taught me that personal charm is insufficient for powerful preaching. A winning smile and witty illustrations are meaningless if you haven't done the hard work of preparing your words and developing your character.

Communal Training

If the first model of the preacher as coach is the Eli-Samuel model, the second is the Elijah-Elisha model. To be sure, there's still a strong individual mentoring component to the Elijah-Elisha relationship. In 1 Kings 19:16, God clearly directs Elijah to choose Elisha as his successor: "Anoint Elisha son of Shaphat from Abel Meholah to succeed you as prophet."

The Elijah story informs us God is actively involved in the transition process. In a deeply distressing moment in Elijah's life (he's overwhelmed and depressed), God says, *I want you to identify and invest in your successor*. And then God graciously gives Elijah a name and an address. Elijah spends the following months and years investing in Elisha.

That said, while Elijah is the most famous prophet in his era, he wasn't a solo act.

We read in 1 Kings 20:41 of an encounter King Ahab has with an unnamed prophet of Israel. The verse says Ahab "recognized him as one of the prophets." During the reign of Ahab then, there was a group; a team of prophets operating in concert with one another.

So, while younger prophet-preachers like Samuel and Elisha received individual coaching, there's also a collective group of prophets who are committed to mutual encouragement and learning. Second Kings reveals Elijah was a part of a company of prophets, not a lone ranger.

On the day Elijah ascends to heaven in a whirlwind, groups of prophets in both Bethel and Jericho tell Elisha this will be his last day with his master. And after Elijah disappears, the company of prophets in Jericho mobilize 50 of their men as a search party to locate Elijah. Later in Elisha's story we read that he is still functioning as part of a group. Second Kings 9:1, 4 says, "The prophet Elisha summoned a man from the company of the prophets. . . . So the young prophet went to Ramoth Gilead."

This model isn't unique to Elisha. Hundreds of years later in Israel's history, the people of God return from the exile in Babylon. Even then, a group of prophets comes alongside Zerubbabel and Joshua to support them in their work (see the prophecies in Haggai and Zechariah).

The Hebrew prophet model has preachers working together in community: sharing responsibilities, coaching younger preachers, and coordinating strategic ministry. I experienced some of my most transformational growth as a preacher as part of a "company of preachers."

At 25, I planted a church in suburban Detroit. I quickly learned I couldn't carry the preaching load alone. When we launched, we had two services every week, a Sunday evening discipleship service with expositional preaching and a Thursday night evangelistic service with topical preaching. Before long we were doing multiple services on both nights and eventually added another location.

My copastor, Beau McCarthy, who now leads the church, has his own unique style and approach to preaching. It was a gift not just to have a break from speaking, but also to receive teaching from Scripture from a friend and partner who shared a common desire to see our community transformed. As the church morphed through different iterations and seasons, we sensed we needed to include a plurality of voices beyond just the two of us. At this point, Caren Hunter began preaching with us as well. Caren was already a part of our church, and because she came from a different theological stream from me, she offered valuable feedback on certain doctrinal points I needed to preach with clarity. We weren't strangers cycling through a common pulpit; we were partners serving together in community. Though it's been more than a decade since we worked together, I'd gladly sit under their preaching today.

While I was completing my work in seminary, I learned about a yearlong cohort-based learning track for preachers. The program, called Micah Groups, brings men and women from diverse racial and denominational backgrounds to explore the intersection of preaching, worship, and justice for the city in which they live. I was fortunate enough to participate in two Micah Groups during my time in Metro Detroit.

The first group allowed me to engage with preachers from Presbyterian, Church of Christ, and nondenominational backgrounds. There were no power dynamics; no one reported to anyone else. We were on a shared growth journey together. We had a curriculum that we followed. There were Scripture readings, sermons to listen to, articles and books to read, and a monthly meeting where we often shared Communion. Diallo, Daniel, Sara, and Matt all spoke into my preaching, and I'm better because of it.

The second group was comprised of a group of emerging teachers at a large suburban church. I facilitated this group with my colleague, Danny Cox. Because the church was a multisite church, we had participants from different locations and different departments. We had male and female voices from a variety of church backgrounds and one participant from South Africa. Though I had more years preaching than others in that particular group, we functioned as a company of preachers/prophets and together asked challenging questions about what it meant for our church to be a prophetic voice in our context in a unique chapter of its history. I still count Michelle Erickson, Michelle Rohner, Michelle Robertson, Danny Cox, Mike Mulliniks, Adam Smart, Michael Bouchard, Adrienne Asher, and Bryon Rossi as friends and mentors.

Maximizing Ministry

The preacher as coach is exhilarated by preachers who go beyond what he or she could do. Jesus spends three years investing in his company of apostles and blesses them, believing and expecting them to do "even greater things" (John 14:12). In his final speech to Peter, he warns him against comparing himself to John, explaining they have specific roles in declaring and advancing the kingdom of God in their lifetimes (John 21:20–23).

In Acts 9, God tells Ananias he is going to play a pivotal role in Paul's spiritual development. We don't know what kind of crash course Ananias gave Paul, but shortly after Ananias baptizes him, Paul is preaching Christ as Lord in the Damascus synagogues. Ananias is but a footnote in church history. Paul goes on to get top billing as a formative voice shaping the early church throughout the Mediterranean.

In Acts 18, when Apollos, an Egyptian follower of Jesus with Jewish roots, arrives in Ephesus, he's already an accomplished preacher in his own right. Even so, Aquilla and Priscilla, refugees from Rome, "invited him to their home and explained to him the way of God more adequately" (Acts 18:26). Aquilla and Priscilla are never noted for their skill in preaching, but Apollos only gets better because of their investment in him.

Finally, Paul's investment in Timothy and Titus, as leaders and preachers, has already been covered well by others, but are further examples of Paul's commitment to the preacher as coach model.

The preacher as coach helps us move from the temptation to cement our legacy to the mandate to maximize ministry. When preaching is by, for, and about us, we are tempted to identify and create preaching clones, people who preach the kinds of things we would preach in the way that we would preach them. But the goal of developing emerging preachers is to empower and release them into their unique callings using their distinct voices.

Insecure preachers want to keep emerging voices on a short leash, for fear they might be eclipsed by a rising star. The "company of prophets" model insulates us from this mentality. It reminds us that we are hearing and speaking the words of God together and that our community is enriched by our collective experience and complementary gifts.

8

The Preacher As Joy-Generator

There's a phrase in Mark's gospel that always leaps out at me. Jesus is teaching in Jerusalem, and the writer captures the people's response to his message. Mark 12:37 says, "The large crowd listened to him with delight."

When I was a child, I had a picture Bible. And whenever Jesus was preaching to the masses, the images focused on Jesus. The crowd was a blur of nameless, faceless robed figures. I never seemed to grasp what they were sensing or feeling. Sometimes, when I read of the events leading up to Christ's death, it seems because of the lack of a crowd that people had ignored or rejected his message. And many did.

John 6:66 describes a moment where, in response to Jesus' teaching, "many of his disciples turned back and no longer followed him." And some preachers cling to this image as they consider their audiences. Effective preaching, they say, will result in people rejecting our message. There's a school of preaching that says, "If people aren't leaving your church offended, you're not preaching the gospel."

Preaching sometimes means declaring hard truths that may drive listeners away. But not always. There should be as many, if not more, moments when people listen to us with delight, just like Jesus' audience in the temple courts.

Delight in Preaching

Delight. It's not often a word people associate with hearing, or even giving, a sermon. But if we miss delight in preaching, it becomes rote for the preacher and stale for the hearer. So, in addition to all the other roles preachers play, let me add "joy-generator" to the list.

The angel who declared Christ's birth to shepherds near Bethlehem said, "Do not be afraid. I bring you good news that will cause great joy for all the people" (Luke 2:10). When the shepherds rushed into town to relay the news, I imagine them running with delight. Joyful messages are most credible when delivered by joyful messengers.

There were moments in my early ministry days when my preaching was marked by pressure. I felt the gravity and responsibility to get the text "right" and to get the delivery "right." Every message felt like a mix between a job interview and a final exam. I can't help but wonder if the audience, either consciously or unconsciously, picked up on my anxiousness. In the past few years, I discovered the critical distinction between the duty of preaching and the delight in preaching.

If I'm not careful, I can pursue preaching as a vehicle for validation. The pulpit can become a showcase to affirm my worth, wit, and way with words. But it's a dangerous dance. Personal insecurity prompts me to leverage preaching for me, not for the good of the hearer. Over time, seeking validation through preaching can push us to crave new venues, new accolades, or an expanded sphere of influence. If we don't name and wrestle down the unintentional desire to use preaching for validation, preaching becomes a drug we require, rather than a gift we offer.

Preaching from delight, however, is an avenue for worship. This has been the most helpful way for me to frame my preaching. It's not a moment where I function as proxy for a distant deity; it's an intimate act of engaging with God in the preaching moment itself. Preaching is the moment in which I feel nearest to God. It's personal. It's energizing. And yes, it's laced with joy.

Eric Liddell, the runner who won gold in the 400 meters at the 1924 Olympics said, "God made me fast. And when I run, I feel His pleasure." The same should be true of our preaching. When we preach, we should feel his pleasure. And that joy should be evident in our faces and in our tone. It's taken me some time to see preaching in this light, and my journey is by no means complete. But I knew I was experiencing a shift in my perspective when I would connect with members of our church in the lobby after a service. If someone was complimentary about a particular sermon, I noticed myself replying, "Thank you. I have so much fun doing it."

When the preacher is a joy-generator, everybody, the preacher included, feels it. So what sparks this joy? The arc of Scripture tells us joy is born from delight in the Word, God's presence, and service.

Delight in the Word

In the chapter "Preacher as Listener," I spoke about how a steady diet of Scripture helps us hear God's voice. Yet, there's a distinction between hearing God's truth and delighting in it.

The psalmist declares, "Blessed is the one . . . whose delight is in the law of the Lord" (Ps. 1:1–2).

I can read the Bible devotionally as a habit. I can consume the text in the study as a part of my vocation. I can do both of these regularly and still fail to delight in it. Some of us need to reclaim or rediscover the joy that comes with engaging the Word for its own sake, not because we have to or are supposed to.

Psalm 119:103 shouts, "How sweet are your words to my taste, sweeter than *honey* to my mouth!" (emphasis added). Ancient cultures didn't have processed sugar. Their only chance to taste something sweet was organic honey. And it was delectable. Apparently, the psalmist never passed on a chance for spiritual or culinary sweetness.

What's true for the psalmists is true for Paul. He says, "Love . . . rejoices with the truth" (1 Cor. 13:6). In his letter to the church in Rome, he writes, "in my inner being I delight in God's law" (Rom. 7:22). Delighting in the Word, then, stretches us as people of love, truth, and joy. We can't expect to generate joy in preaching the text if we don't delight in the text for its own sake.

Delight in God's Presence

The psalmist also reminds us that delight isn't just found in the principles of the text, but in the person behind them. It's possible to believe there's value in God's presence but miss the delight found there.

The songwriter calls us to "Take delight in the Lord, and he will give you the desires of your heart" (Ps. 37:4) and declares, "The Lord makes firm the steps of the one who delights in him" (Ps. 37:23). If the preacher is called to spark joy in the hearts of hearers, he or she must display the fruit of intimate time spent in God's presence.

Based on our personal wiring and faith traditions, we experience God's presence in distinct ways. It's critical for you to understand which rhythms and practices allow you to dwell in God's presence. That said, silence and solitude are staples for preachers and leaders throughout Scripture. The lives of Moses, David, Elijah, Jonah, Anna, John the Baptist, Jesus, Ananias, and Paul are all marked by moments of withdrawal from work and public ministry for times of reflection and prayer.

The voice of wisdom, captured in Proverbs 8:30, says, "Then I was constantly at his side. I was filled with delight day after day, rejoicing always in his presence." Preachers who delight in God's presence for the sole purpose of intimate connection with God sound different than those who tick off a perfunctory "check-in with God" before preaching. A deep, inner life that is marked by the Spirit's fruit, with joy among them, cannot be faked. It's real or it's not. Our preaching flows out of either the depths of our engagement with God or the shallows of it.

While preaching at Pentecost, Peter quotes Psalm 16:11 to describe Jesus: "You make known to me the path of life; you will fill me with joy in your presence." Peter is a first-hand witness to the joy Jesus modeled as he walked with and spent time with the Father. It's only as we delight in God's presence that we can authentically invite others to do the same.

Delight in Service

Whatever joy we find in the text and in the presence of God we carry with us into the pulpit. Jeremiah says, "When your words came, I ate them; they were my joy and my heart's delight, for I bear your name, Lord God Almighty" (Jer. 15:16). This confession doesn't mean Jeremiah's preaching was lighthearted. They don't call him "the weeping prophet" for nothing. Still, by Jeremiah's own admission, hearing God's Word was a reason for delight. If hearing God's truth is delightful, then transmitting that truth is also energizing. The weeping comes when the people God loves, and we love, fail to appreciate it for what it is: a path to life.

John the Baptist is another case study here. When John was baptizing people at Aenon near Salim, he told his disciples, "The friend who attends the bridegroom waits and listens for him, and is full of joy when he hears the bridegroom's voice. That joy is mine, and it is now complete. He must become greater; I must become less" (John 3:29–30). As a preacher, John knows his role is to point to a person greater than himself. Hearing Christ's voice fills him with joy, and directing his audience to Jesus is undeniably life-giving for him.

John's legacy challenges me to ask myself, "When I step into the preaching moment, is my joy complete? Is my message flowing out of an abundance of joy? Or am I running a deficit?"

When Joy Is Absent

But life isn't always delightful. There are challenges and heartbreaks and setback for both the preacher and the people of God. When Nehemiah had Ezra read the Book of the Law to the exiles returning from Babylon, the people were overwhelmed, shell-shocked. They had no idea how far they had strayed from God's truth and design for them. When they heard the words of Ezra and the Levites, they began to weep with sorrow.

Nehemiah's response? He doesn't command them to grovel; he invites them to reset, physically and spiritually. In Nehemiah 8:10 he says, "Go and enjoy choice food and sweet drinks, and send some to those who have nothing prepared. This day is holy to our Lord. Do not grieve, for the joy of the Lord is your strength." On a holy day, choice food will nourish their bodies and the deep joy will refresh their souls.

Nehemiah, as preacher, acknowledges the gravity of the moment. The people are awake to the sins they've committed in ignorance, individually and collectively. Nehemiah doesn't deny it. Yet, he knows confession opens the door to repentance, which leads to restoration. And restoration is marked by joy and results in strength.

The preacher as joy-generator names where joy is absent and gently redirects the people of God back to the author and sustainer of joy.

Joy Killers

If delight is the hallmark of a preacher's life and work, then why does so much of our preaching feel joyless, either to us or our hearers? I can trace this back to fatigue, resentment, and grief in my own life.

Fatigue

Preaching fatigue is real. I don't think preachers who are tempted to plagiarize are necessarily lazy—I think they're tired. Tired of generating new content, tired of finding new illustrations, tired of the grind, or exhausted by the potential monotony of Sunday mornings that never stop coming.

As a church planter in my mid-20s, I felt like I had enough adrenaline to preach for a lifetime. But then the church grew and changed, and then plateaued. Some close friends left. Staff left. And more came. The transient nature of our community meant as soon as you started to connect with a family, their job or circumstances took them to Chicago, Los Angeles, or Nashville.

I got married. And Kelly and I navigated new rhythms of her finishing school and starting a job as a full-time nurse. For a season she worked the midnight shift, and it was hard for us to see each other regularly. Then we had a daughter, and another daughter, and a son, and a third daughter. And the preaching that was once so life-giving sometimes felt like a drain. I felt like all my discretionary time and money was escaping my grasp like water through my fingers.

It was sometime in this season that a mentor told me, "Steve, the church will never say 'no' for you." He's right. It won't. The job is not an energy-sucking black hole, but it's an insatiable role. It will eat as much as we feed it. I've had friends and colleagues who are in a constant state of exhaustion. I'll ask, "Why do you work 60-, 70-, 80-hour weeks? Is your congregation asking you to do this?" They'll say, "No. That's just what it takes to get the job done." They're wrong. The job is to serve the people of God well. We cannot serve them with joy when we're running on fumes.

As preachers, we can only give away what we possess. If exhaustion is stealing your joy, it's time to steal it back. If you're struggling with being addicted to, or codependent with, your ministry role, consider reading *The Emotionally Healthy Leader: How Transforming Your Inner Life Will Deeply Transform Your Church, Team, and the World* by Peter Scazzero. Take time to review how your sleep patterns, eating habits, and exercise routines are adding or subtracting energy in your life.

Resentment

Physical and vocational fatigue cause joy leaks. But unaddressed emotional and spiritual issues do too. For me, resentment became my chief joy thief. Fatigue can be experienced early in ministry, but resentment seems to build over time. Like plaque hardening on arteries pumping oxygen from the heart, resentment clogs our spiritual pipelines. It hinders the movement of joy—in and through us.

I've tasted resentment toward individuals, institutions, churches, ideologies, strangers, and even God. Some resentment can be traced back to personal slights and very real wounds. Other threads go back to unaddressed heartaches or traumas that may predate our work as preachers. I don't know where your resentment of others may lie—their offenses, indifference, or success—but I know this: resentment is a threat to joy.

The only remedy is to actively cultivate a spirit of mercy and a heart of gratitude. Jesus' prayer "Father, forgive them, for they do not know what they are doing" (Luke 23:34) has been a lifeline for me. I've wasted years thinking former leaders, friends, or supervisors intentionally set out to harm me and undermine my influence. Remembering that many harmed me out of ignorance, and that I have harmed others in ignorance, gives me traction on my forgiveness journey.

The medicine for resentment is a daily dose of gratitude. Gratitude reminds us of all that we have that we didn't win, earn, or deserve. A few years ago, I participated in a spiritual formation initiative. One of the exercises was to record 10 different items for which we were thankful every day for 21 days. It was transformative. I don't have to tell you my "joy meter" was in a far healthier place at the end of the exercise than it was in the beginning.

Grief

Fatigue and resentment hinder joy. However, if we're attentive, we can head them off at the pass. You can address short-term fatigue with a nap, retreat, or vacation. You can stem the tide of resentment with confession, repentance, making amends, and expressing gratitude. There are firewalls you can construct to defend against fatigue and resentment.

But you can't defend against grief. Loss, trauma, and disappointment are rarely predictable. Grief is the tsunami that levels any semblance of normal. Grief shatters delight.

I walked with a preacher through the dissolution of his marriage. It wasn't what he wanted and he couldn't stop it. The grief born out of the rejection, betrayal, and abandonment was overwhelming. I witnessed a preacher experience rejection over her gifting. It wasn't that the church she was preaching for in a volunteer capacity didn't value woman as preachers; they just never affirmed her as a preacher. It was heartbreaking. I've tasted grief myself in losing my father and in being passed over for a ministry role I'd pursued for years.

In the wake of grief, it's difficult to preach with joy. It looks ridiculous as I write it. It's an absurd understatement. But sometimes

Sunday comes anyway. Sometimes the people know of our grief and they extend grace to us. Sometimes we can't or don't tell them. We soldier on, suffering in silence.

Psalm 137:1-3 says, "By the rivers of Babylon we sat and wept when we remembered Zion. There on the poplars we hung our harps, for there our captors asked us for songs, our tormentors demanded songs of joy; they said, 'Sing us one of the songs of Zion!'" Grief can paralyze us. It tightens our throats and squeezes our chests when we're supposed to preach. We don't know what to say or do. But the moment calls us to preach anyway.

I don't have a formula for how to preach in and through grief. A full year after my father's death and years after a moment of ministry disappointment, I'm still figuring it out myself. All I know is that the gospel invites me to view every loss through the lens of the Resurrection, to believe that the sting we feel in loss will be reversed at a future date. If Christ is indeed the resurrection and the life, I can choose to believe (and invite others to believe), that he can, does, and will redeem all things for his glory.

Grief then, is a chapter in our story. But not the last one. The psalmist reminds us, "Those who go out weeping, carrying seed to sow, will return with songs of joy, carrying sheaves with them" (Ps. 126:6). We may sow in sorrow, but we will reap with joy, if not on this side of eternity, then surely on the other side.

May you, preacher, delight in receiving spiritual truths, and may your hearers delight in receiving spiritual truths.

9

The Preacher As Pipeline

Raise your hand if you've heard this one before: "Preach the gospel at all times; use words if necessary." Somewhere along the way, this maxim was attributed to Francis of Assisi, even though it's apocryphal. In a piece debunking the quote, Glenn Stanton says, "The closest [sentiment] comes from his Rule of 1221, Chapter XII on how the Franciscans should practice their preaching:

> No brother should preach contrary to the form and regulations of the holy Church nor unless he has been permitted by his minister . . . All the Friars . . . should preach by their deeds.[1]

So, while Assisi doesn't endorse a wordless gospel, he does call preachers to live their message daily. Of course, it's easier to declare the gospel than it is to live it, but preaching requires both: that we proclaim spiritual life and act as pipelines through which that life flows.

[1] Glen Stanton, "Fact Checker: Misquoting Francis of Assisi," The Gospel Coalition (July 10, 2012). Accessed on November 3, 2020. https://www.thegospelcoalition.org/article/factchecker-misquoting-francis-of-assisi/.

'The Preachers'

Western Michigan has a unique art scene. The city of Grand Rapids hosts Art Prize, a regular citywide display of two-dimensional, three-dimensional, time-based, and installation pieces. Since Art Prize began, thousands of artists have displayed artwork and millions of visitors have come to see it. In 2018, I entered a piece called "The Preachers." With the help of my talented friend Bob, I built a simple wooden pulpit and a matching six-foot pew. The exhibit was an interactive experiment where I, the "reverend," invited strangers to come and "preach" to me. They could present planned or spontaneous remarks. It was a fascinating and eye-opening experience.

When Art Prize was over, I took the collapsible pew and put it in my garage. The pulpit, however, was a little cumbersome, so I put it in my office at the church. Because I announced my departure from the church about a month before I preached for the last time as the paid teaching pastor, I was able to move out of my church office in phases. Every day over the course of four weeks I put another few boxes into my car after work and brought them home.

My last day at the church was Thursday, January 30 of 2018. On that day, I loaded up my remaining odds and ends into a cardboard box and took them down to my car. Then it was time to claim the lone remaining object from the office: my pulpit. I carried it down the stairs to the parking lot and set it down behind my car so I could put it in the trunk.

I remember standing there for a moment, just staring at it. The pulpit in the parking lot. A simple portable wooden lectern I could take with me wherever I went.

That image continues to be a gift to me. It reminds me that my preaching, and yours, isn't fixed. It's not anchored in a building, nor tethered to a fixed time or place. That may be true of our jobs, or our platforms in a given community. But my calling as a preacher doesn't hinge on pastorates or platforms. It turns on my desire and ability to steward my voice for God's glory.

Not a Bucket Passer, But a Conduit

I'm often tempted to view preaching as the transfer of spiritual information. I can imagine the gospel like water in a bucket for a fire brigade. I see a black and white film of villagers passing one pail feverishly to the next person in line, with the last person throwing water at a burning barn. Sometimes I see my preaching as a part of a fire brigade, hoping the water I throw will quench the flames of ignorance. But if there's a hole in the bucket or failure in the water-throwing technique, the fire rages on and we start all over again. It can feel futile. It's a depressing way to view a beautiful responsibility.

But there's another way to see the preacher—not as bucket passer, but as a conduit, a pipeline through which life-giving water never stops flowing. In John 4:14, Jesus says, "Whoever drinks the water I give them will never thirst. Indeed, the water I give them will become in them a spring of water welling up to eternal life." He repeats this theme, in John 7:38, "Whoever believes in me, as Scripture has said, rivers of living water will flow from within them." This image, of Jesus' disciples acting as a pipeline for spiritual vitality, isn't unique to preachers, but it certainly applies to them as well.

The preacher as pipeline is an ever-present channel through which the message of Jesus flows. He or she is always on the ready to preach in the moment, on the move, and by the Spirit. According to Jesus, opportunities to speak on his behalf are predictably unpredictable, so the preacher must always be prepared to present.

In the Moment

Jesus told his disciples there would be times when they would be called on to speak without warning: "Whenever you are arrested and brought to trial, do not worry beforehand about what to say. Just say whatever is given you at the time, for it is not you speaking, but the Holy Spirit" (Mark 13:11). There will be moments, of crisis or opportunity, when our preaching will be impromptu, spontaneous. In those times, our words will come through the prompting of the Spirit and out of the depth of our intimacy with Christ.

There's a story about a young man who is impressed by an eloquent speaker (in some versions it's a preacher; in others it's a statesman). The young man approaches the communicator after the speech and asks, "How long did it take you to write that talk?" and the speaker responds, "I've been writing this message my whole life." The same is true for the preacher as pipeline.

When there is actually no time to prepare, we know that the Spirit speaks for us and draws from the years of experience and learning leading up to this moment. Peter's message at Pentecost was one such moment. It was incredibly effective. Thousands of people responded to a gospel message that Peter never wrote down in advance.

The same is true for Stephen. When his accusers haul him before the Sanhedrin, there's no time for him to prepare his thoughts. But he gives a thorough defense of the gospel. And it's not just his words that are moving; it's his physical demeanor as well. Acts 6:15 tells us, "All who were sitting in the Sanhedrin looked intently at Stephen, and they saw that his face was like the face of an angel." The light in Stephen's eyes isn't something he's consciously planned. It's the obvious overflow of the power of God at work within him.

On the Move

If the preacher should be prepared to speak anytime, he or she should also be ready to speak anywhere, from temple courts to private homes and everywhere in between. Sometimes it means being a roadside evangelist. Acts 8:4 tells us, "Those who had been scattered preached the word wherever they went." Philip "started out, and on his way he met an Ethiopian eunuch . . ." (8:27). Persecution forced Philip out of his "pulpit." Now he's free to preach anywhere, and he does.

In another life, Philip likely wouldn't have imagined preaching in Samaritan villages, and certainly not in a foreign official's chariot, but as a pipeline, he's ready to preach to anyone, anywhere, at any time. This the privilege we have as preachers: the honor of being present at the crossroads of others' lives, even when those are literal crossroads.

By the Spirit

The common thread behind preaching anytime and anywhere is the Holy Spirit. The Spirit initiates the moment and influences the outcome. When Peter defends his visit to the Gentiles to the church in Jerusalem, he says, "As I began to speak, the Holy Spirit came on them as he had come on us at the beginning" (Acts 11:15). Even if Peter didn't fully understand the events leading up to his preaching at Cornelius' house, the Spirit's influence on the hearing confirmed God was present and working in that moment.

When we examine Paul and Barnabas' ministry, we see similar, undeniable spiritual evidence that God is working through them. Acts 14:3 says, "So Paul and Barnabas spent considerable time there, speaking boldly for the Lord, who confirmed the message of his grace by enabling them to perform signs and wonders."

Paul doesn't see himself as a preaching savant, though he was schooled in both theology and rhetoric. Rather, Paul self-identifies as a channel through which the Spirit moves. In his first letter to the Corinthians he writes, "My message and my preaching were not with wise and persuasive words, but with a demonstration of the Spirit's power" (2:4) and "For the kingdom of God is not a matter of talk but of power" (4:20).

Paul encourages Timothy to think this way as well, reminding him that it's possible to have a "form of godliness but [deny] its power" (2 Tim. 3:5). Timothy's first task is to walk in, and be available to, the Spirit. If he connects regularly with Jesus, his life and ministry will be marked with spiritual influence.

The preacher-as-pipeline motif has been life giving for me personally. It permits me to see preaching as a service that transcends specific roles, times, and places. When a river of life surges through preachers, it touches everyone around them. The prophet Ezekiel tells of a life-giving stream filled with water that "flows toward the eastern region and goes down into the Arabah, where it enters the Dead Sea. When it empties into the sea, the salty water there becomes fresh. Swarms of living creatures will live wherever the river flows" (Ezek. 47:8–9). It's my prayer that, as you are a conduit for the gospel, spiritual life would flourish wherever your words land.

The Shrinking Sea

If you ever have a chance to visit Israel or Jordan, one of the must-see stops is the Dead Sea. But if you stay at one of the many resorts along the world's most salty body of water, you'll see something odd. Some of the boardwalks that lead from the hotels to the beach stop more than a hundred yards before the shoreline. The reason? The Dead Sea is dying; it's literally shrinking. Fresh water is such a precious resource in the Middle East that the Israelis and Jordanians siphon water from the Jordan River as it flows from the mountains north of Galilee.

While the source of the Jordan—mountain springs, rain, and snowmelt—is steady, the conduit is fragile. And when the Jordan's flow is hindered, the Dead Sea pays the price.

As preachers, the Source of our joy and vitality is faithful. When we align our minds and step with the Spirit, the fruit of love, peace, gentleness, and kindness are undeniable. And yet, if your life is anything like mine, the water I receive at the spring doesn't always make its way down the sea. Dwight L. Moody said, "The fact is, we are leaky vessels, and we have to keep right under the fountain all the time to keep full of Christ, and so have fresh supply."[2]

Are there times, places, or triggers where you feel like a leaky conduit? Are you delivering a trickle instead of a torrent?

Is it possible that, even though your devotional life and prep times are happening as they should, something seems out of kilter? And, at the end of the day, the message you're preaching both in and out of the pulpit feels flat?

Then stay close to Christ, our living water, and look for patterns or themes around the "leaks." If you're still stuck, consider asking for help on some spiritual diagnostics.

Plumbers sometimes put a non-staining dye in pipelines to check for leaks. Over the years, I've learned to trust the insights of those who love me enough to run "dye tests," whether I've asked them to or not. Whether it's my wife, Kelly, noting that I snapped at one of our kids, or my daughter observing that I've gone from "zero to one hundred" in my impatience, those in my closest circle are my best "leak detectors." They remind me that I can't expect to be a solid conduit on Sunday if I'm hemorrhaging the peace of Christ on Thursday afternoon.

Sometimes re-engaging in spiritual practices allows us to patch the pipeline. But sometimes the holes require a master welder. If you've never reached out to a counselor, a spiritual director, or a recovery sponsor, cracks in the conduit are compelling reasons to do so. It takes courage to start these conversations, but I'm finding the work is always worth it.

---

[2] Dwight L. Moody, *The Secret of Success in the Christian Life* (Chicago: Moody Publishers, 2001), 37.

10

The Preacher As Fellow Sufferer

I heard an ad on the radio for a physician with a solution for people suffering from nerve pain in their hands and feet. The tag line for the ad was: "Imagine living pain free for the rest of your life." If you're struggling with chronic pain, you're ready to pick up the phone. You'll do anything to escape the gnawing ache, the needling discomfort.

Oftentimes the preacher helps a church navigate a church crisis, a community crisis, or a national crisis. Shepherding a community through moments of pain and suffering requires focus and intentionality.

When I served at a large suburban church near Detroit, we had a mantra when we prepared for our weekend services and when we debriefed conversations with people in crisis—"Never underestimate the pain in the room." On any given Sunday, the odds that at least one person in your sanctuary is struggling with loss, heartache, rejection, loneliness, or failure is 100 percent.

The husband who wandered in because his wife just served him with divorce papers is yearning for consolation. A young man recently arrested for his second DUI is scrambling to escape the maze of addiction. A couple lost their infant daughter to SIDS. A high school senior was rejected by her first-choice college. A family is facing foreclosure. The grief is suffocating. But every week they come. Familiar faces with old wounds. New faces with fresh scars. All pushing the pain just deep enough to hide from the most discerning eyes.

To acknowledge all that suffering, we need to make the pulpit a mirror (a reminder not to live in denial of the brokenness) and a beacon (pointing to Christ's faithfulness and care as we navigate dark valleys together).

Even the most broken of preachers steps into the pulpit with the desire to serve brokenhearted people. No one would ever confuse me for the most empathetic person they know, but I cling to the truth of Psalm 34:18: "The Lord is close to the *brokenhearted* and saves those who are crushed in spirit" (emphasis added). My great hope is that those who are emotionally, physically, and spiritually injured would find healing and encouragement in real-time encounters with Christ. I come from a faith tradition where we believe that God can and does dramatically heal people. I still believe this. At the same time, I've seen Jesus-honoring, Bible-believing, Spirit-led, faith-filled people breathe their last breath with their healing prayer unanswered. So how, in our preaching, do we reconcile the wish for pain-free living with the ever-present weight of suffering?

Three Approaches to Human Suffering

At the risk of oversimplifying a complex issue, allow me to present three approaches to human suffering: escape, tolerate, and redeem. In the first approach, escapists reject suffering in all its forms. They don't deny that pain exists; they discount it as a lack of faith. The argument goes: "Christ healed the sick, diseased, and oppressed in his time and also does in ours. God's intent for us is pain-free living, and if we're stuck in some kind of agony, something is broken on our end—not God's. Increased faith and an upward tick in moral performance insures a pain-free existence." The injunction for those suffering? Try harder; the burden for escaping hurt rests solely on your shoulders. If you've been in church circles long enough, you've heard a version of this view.

The second approach, tolerate, avoids the aforementioned escapism. The adherents of this view consider themselves realists. This theory contends: "The Fall introduced brokenness in the world. We are living in the midst of that fallout. Death, tragedy, and disease are the natural consequences of humanity's first and subsequent rejection of God's will. Followers of Jesus will eventually move beyond this system, either at the point of death or at Christ's return. Nobody's excited about the reality of suffering. It's just something we're stuck with in our current state." The call here? Steel your resolve, stiffen your back, and bite your lip. The waves will keep coming; you just have to do your best to absorb the blows.

Scripture offers a third way: redeem. The writer of Hebrews states, "For the joy set before him he endured the cross, scorning its shame, and sat down at the right hand of the throne of God" (12:2). It's a position on suffering rarely modeled in a pain-avoiding society.

'Joy Set Before Us'

Maybe we rarely embrace this position because we don't have a solid grasp of what the "joy set before us" might look like. But when we do, that joy is a beacon—it lifts us and compels us to take another faithful step forward. Years ago, I was on a teaching team that preached a seven-part series on the life of Paul. In one of the messages, we focused on Paul's understanding of suffering as it shapes the life of the disciple and the church. The apostle Paul had an unambiguous vision for his life, which is why he appears so reckless in the face of very real threats. If anyone has a resume with exhaustive suffering credentials to tout, it's Paul, and he reluctantly declares them in 2 Corinthians 11:23–33.

Have you stopped to reflect on this? Five times Paul gets 40 lashes minus one. He's beaten with rods three times, survives a stoning attempt, and is shipwrecked three times. Apparently, he keeps signing up for this. I got punched in the face in eighth grade and needed five stitches over my eye. Unfortunately, the incident had nothing to do with me being a voice for the gospel, so there wasn't much joy to be had in it.

Our culture is committed to protection, security, and pain avoidance. There's an ongoing debate between law enforcement and large tech companies. It centers on two deeply held American rights: privacy and security. Paul's solution is simple: Surrender both. *I only have one goal: spreading the gospel. You can take everything else.*

Look at how Paul suspends his rights in Acts 16. After he and Silas deliver an unnamed slave girl from a demon, her owners incite a riot. Paul and Silas are beaten and imprisoned without due process. But being in jail isn't necessarily a setback. It's an opportunity. Their midnight worship service declares their faith in Christ to a captive audience. You know the rest—there's an earthquake, a jailer's conversion, and a family baptism in the early morning hours. If Paul and Silas had lawyered up, there never would have been this dramatic jailhouse evangelism moment.

The rest of the story is a moving snapshot of what redemptive, gospel-oriented suffering can do. The morning after their stint in jail, the Philippian magistrates order Paul and Silas' release. Oddly enough, Paul won't leave (Acts 16:37–40).

A colleague of mine once took a church group on a tour to Greece. Their guide on that trip, Kostas, had some fascinating insight on this episode. He contends Paul knew that the judges and jailers didn't have legal standing to arrest, punish, or imprison them. But he let them beat him and hold him anyway. Why? Because Paul knows the fledgling church in Philippi needs all the help it can get. It's small and fragile and needs time and freedom to establish roots. So instead of advocating for his own rights, Paul embraces a punishment he doesn't deserve. In so doing, he mirrors their pain, identifies with their suffering, and names the challenges they face.

Then, rather than suing the municipality for damages, he asks for an escort. In so doing, Paul "buys" political protection for his friends—Lydia, a slave girl, and the unnamed jailer. The unspoken exchange between Paul and local branch of the Roman Empire goes like this: *I'll leave quietly and you'll leave my friends alone.* Paul risked his well-being and personal safety to go to the mat for those he loves.

So Paul's list of horrible experiences isn't a tirade about the nature of evil, the miscarriage of justice, or a quest for self-vindication. It's a celebration of a bold love that embraces suffering for the glory of God and the good of others.

The Reality of Suffering

It would be easy to touch abstractly on the theology of suffering in an overview of Paul's life. But the pain in a congregation, and the prevalence of tragedy in the world, is a daily reality. How do we touch on God's capacity to redeem our personal heartaches and broken dreams for our good and his glory on a regular basis?

As preachers, our job is to champion the value of redemptive suffering at three levels: societal, congregational, and personal. I was just starting to discern my ministry calling in the late '80s and early '90s. At that time there was much discussion about the church's need to be relevant to culture—to see, identify, and relate to the average person's experience and felt needs. It was, and remains, a valid argument. If we can't contextualize our sermons to our audience, there's no incentive for them to listen. But globalization has changed the way people see the world. A generation ago, traditional print and broadcast news limited what messages we received about what was happening in the world. Today, with a 24-hour news cycle and social media, I can hear bad news from any corner of the world in an instant. The challenge for the preacher, then, is how to acknowledge the current events people are struggling to process without regurgitating bad news.

There was a time when people could only grieve about the events that directly affected them. But now, people who show up for the preaching moment are affected by events that also touch them indirectly. As I am writing this chapter, the world is reeling from the global coronavirus pandemic. The scope of the tragedy is staggering. My coworker José lost his uncle in Texas. And my friend Mike recently told me that his friend Jalen personally knows 70 people who were infected and, as of this writing, 21 have passed away.

The Power of Lament

José and Jalen's stories remind me we're not just navigating a global tragedy, but we have an opportunity to learn that there are layers of lament: Some visible crises are stacked atop crises that aren't visible to all. COVID-19 is calling preachers to acknowledge that the disease strikes different communities in different ways; the illness is ravaging neighborhoods that are economically vulnerable. Some have limited access to health care, and the close proximity of housing makes social distancing a challenge.

Some faith traditions are better versed in lament than others. The ones who lament well can do so because they aren't strangers to suffering. Their preaching names heartache, and their liturgies and songs lift their tears to a Messiah who suffered too. In fact, Jesus warns of the danger of ignoring suffering in our broader social context. In Luke 13:1, Jesus hears news of a national tragedy: Pilate had murdered Galileans and mixed their blood with their sacrifices. He responds in verses 2–5:

> Do you think that these Galileans were worse sinners than all the other Galileans because they suffered this way? I tell you, no! But unless you repent, you too will all perish. Or those eighteen who died when the tower in Siloam fell on them—do you think they were more guilty than all the others living in Jerusalem? I tell you, no! But unless you repent, you too will all perish.

For Jesus, tragedy, even if it doesn't directly affect those hearing about it, is a chance to recalibrate, an opportunity to admit the fragility of life and to reject wrong beliefs about God, ourselves, or the lives we live. And the earthly heartache points toward our heavenly hope—the power of the resurrection that anchors us even as grief crashes over us.

The Tension for Preachers

The tension for preachers is how we address events that instill fear in the hearts of some of our members and, at the same time, declare God's power, love, and sovereignty in a broken world. I'm convinced that if we don't regularly admit the prevalence of suffering in our society, our preaching feels tone-deaf to anyone paying attention to the world.

As shepherds who preach, we have the immense privilege of walking with our people through some of their darkest moments. We need to find anchor points in our own pews to shape the conversation about suffering.

I recently met with a woman and her 92-year-old father. He asked for prayer as he faced his fears: the meaning of life, the uncertainty of death, unresolved conflicts among his adult children, and his professional legacy. I woke up another morning to an email informing me that a staff member's mother passed away. If I care for these congregants, and dozens like them, then how do I use the pulpit to mourn with those who mourn (Rom. 12:15)?

When I preach hope or courage or even blessing, how do I frame it in a way that isn't oblivious or contrived to the pain in the pews? Honest, culturally aware preaching recognizes heartache in the world at large, the church family, and ultimately in the preacher's own life.

I know there's an ongoing debate about how much self-revelation is appropriate in our preaching. I'm not convinced that we need to share every setback, slight, and heartache from our personal lives in real time or in full detail. Sometimes, if our tragedy is public, the best approach for ourselves, our families, and our churches is to let other church leaders share difficult news while we take time to process.

But there are other moments when the congregation won't know of particular struggles unless we choose to share them. A few years ago, my wife lost her older sister Kathleen after an extended battle with cancer. She was only 49. For our family, it was important to share our grief with the larger church. It was a unique opportunity for us to invite them into our struggle. Over the next few weeks and months, we were stunned by their compassion and generosity. To share our own hurts, when appropriate, allows the people we lead to see that we are preaching from our own suffering, rather than around it.

Last year I was scheduled to speak on Father's Day. A few weeks before, my 82-year-old dad went to the emergency room in suburban Chicago. He'd been battling a strange infection and had chronic pain in his right arm and hand. After a few days, he rebounded and was admitted to a rehabilitation facility. My family was in Chicago for a wedding, so we visited him on the way to the ceremony. While he seemed weak, he was in good spirits. We all hoped he was turning the corner.

It didn't last. By the second week of June, he was in the intensive care unit. I didn't know if he would make it until Father's Day, so I arranged a backup speaker if things took a turn for the worse. On Father's Day, I did my regular pre-preaching routine. I sat quietly in a room off of the auditorium with my sermon notes. I paused for a moment to collect my thoughts. And then the dam broke. I buried my head in my hands and called Kelly. "I don't think I can do it today," I said through tears. Kelly listened and encouraged me and asked if she should call a friend to assist. After a minute, I was able to collect myself and preach at both services. As a part of the sermon, I acknowledged what our family was going through and identified one of the great gifts my dad gave his children: modeling consistent and faith-filled prayer.

Immediately after the service, I drove just over two hours to Chicago with my family to be with my mom, my siblings, and my dad. It was the last time we would speak. He passed the following Sunday afternoon, surrounded by his family.

As much as we preach to others in their pain, we need our communities to "preach" to us in our own suffering. Their listening, their prayer, their support, and their mourning is a lived sermon of solidarity and community. There are moments when preaching in and through our pain is cathartic for us and a unique gift to our church. Yet, there are other moments when we need to yield the pulpit to other trusted voices so we can be fully present to our own struggle.

Suffering is a constant reality for preachers in the world, in the church, in our own lives. Our instinct is to avoid it at every turn, insulating ourselves and those we love from the anguish. But Scripture reminds us that self-protection is rooted in fear. Redemptive suffering is firmly anchored in faith and love.

So let the pulpit be a mirror—a reminder that people don't have to live in denial of brokenness—and a beacon—pointing to Christ's faithfulness and care as we navigate dark valleys together.

Conclusion

A Box of Hats

Business writer Edward de Bono wrote a book on corporate decision-making called *Six Thinking Hats*. De Bono calls on teams to use different "hats" or perspectives at precise moments in the strategic planning process. These hats, he contends, help executive teams avoid getting stuck or resorting to groupthink.

In a similar vein, I want you take the ten roles explored in this book and "wear" them at specific points in your preaching process. There will be days when you feel stuck as you prepare for a sermon. And there will be days when you feel incapacitated in your calling. Before you spend too much mental energy asking what to do, I want you to remember who you are.

You are a student of Scripture. The biblical record of preaching stands above the style du jour, the current ministry trends, or the whimsy of culture. The Bible reminds us God uses ordinary and flawed people to declare the majesty and mystery of the gospel. Sometimes you'll forget that this hat is critical. There's always time to come back to it.

You are a child of God. Your calling is hardwired into you. You preach because others are tempted to wander from their identity.

You are a fellow traveler, walking and calling your hearers to put one foot in front of the other, one day at a time.

You are a listener inviting others to join you to hear the heartbeat of heaven.

You are an intercessor, mirroring the work of the Spirit, who prays for you even as you lift the people of God in prayer.

You are an artist, weaving and molding words, experience, and declared truth in a beautiful work that encourages, corrects, and rebukes.

You are a coach, privileged with opportunities to help others discover and develop their proclamation gifts.

You are a joy generator, creating space for transcendent delight that will strengthen those with weary arms and weak knees.

You are a pipeline, a conduit through which life-giving refreshment flows.

You are a shepherd, an often-bruised fellow sufferer who, like Jesus, learns and teaches obedience born out of trials.

It's going to take some time and practice to remember and toggle between these roles. You'll have some days when you wear multiple hats in a single sitting. And you'll have seasons when one hat is all you'll need.

In time, you can resist the temptation to focus on how "good" any given sermon is, was, or will be because, "Once you have found the work you are meant to do, the particulars of any single piece don't matter all that much."[1]

Your preaching is a gift, but the greater gift is your life.

---

[1]Dave Bayles and Ted Orland, *Art and Fear: Observations on the Perils (and Rewards) of Artmaking* (Santa Cruz, CA: The Image Continuum, 1993), 62.

Made in the USA
Columbia, SC
16 April 2022